Come to the Table

Healing from the Past, Discovering Purpose in the Present

A Christian Woman's Journey to
Restoration and Redemption

By

Tabitha Morrow

Copyright © 2023

All rights reserved.

All rights reserved. No part of this publication may be reproduced, distributed, or transmitted in any form or by any means, including photocopying, recording, or other electronic or mechanical methods, without the prior written permission of the publisher, except in the case of brief quotations embodied in critical reviews and certain other noncommercial uses permitted by copyright law.
This book is a work of nonfiction. The author has made every effort to ensure the accuracy of the information herein. However, the author and publisher assume no responsibility for errors, omissions, or damages caused by the use of the information contained herein.

Cover design: Isabella Morrow

Printed in the United States

Published By: Tabitha Morrow, Ten27 Living LLC

For questions, contact: shebloomsagency@gmail.com

DEDICATION

This book is lovingly dedicated to the incredible women who have carried the weight of brokenness for far too long. It's for those who've embarked on a journey to discover their true identity, seeking a haven of love and belonging.

I extend my heartfelt gratitude to everyone who played a role in the creation of this book — my dear friends whose prayers and encouragement sustained me, my trusted mentors, and most importantly, my beloved husband and children. Your unwavering love, steadfast faith in me, and unwavering support have been the cornerstone of my strength throughout this incredible journey.

Come to the Table

In a world where past hurts scar and shattered dreams weigh heavy, it's easy to lose sight of who you were meant to be. Yet, deep within your soul, there's a glimmer of hope—an invitation to come to the table and experience profound healing, restoration, and redemption.

Welcome to *Come to the Table: Healing from the Past, Discovering Purpose in the Present.* As you journey through this book and the guided journal reflections and gain profound insights, I pray that you will be led on a soul-stirring discovery toward restoration and redemption found in your true identity in Christ. It's an invitation to shed the weight of labels, pain, and past experiences that hindered your growth and kept you from fully embracing the unique person God created you to be.

Within these pages, you'll step onto a healing path, uncovering your inherent worth as a cherished child of God. Each person is fearfully and wonderfully made, intentionally designed for a divine purpose awaiting your embrace. Immersing yourself in God's Word, you'll dismantle false narratives and cast aside negative self-perceptions, allowing your true identity in Christ to radiate.

This transformative book delves into the power of forgiveness—the balm that heals past wounds—and the art of finding peace and rest in God's comforting presence. It speaks to common struggles like self-doubt, shame, and feeling lost, offering solace, hope, and gentle guidance for those who've temporarily forgotten who they are.

At its core, *Come to the Table* extends an open-hearted invitation to you, urging you to take your rightful place at God's table—an intimate space where you're unconditionally accepted, valued, and wrapped in divine love. This book empowers you to rise above the voices that cloud your true identity and embrace liberating freedom, purpose, and joy in your God-given calling.

The essence of this transformative message lies in the belief that, through this journey of restoration and redemption, you'll experience profound healing, discover your true identity, and unlock the door to a life of purpose rooted in your unbreakable relationship with God. This book stands as a resounding call to reclaim your true self, find healing from past pain, and step into the abundant life that God has lovingly prepared for you as you come to the table.

TABLE OF CONTENTS

Before You Begin	1
Chapter 1: The Table of Unveiling: Bringing Darkness to the Light	8
Journal Reflection: Finding Healing and Restoration	17
Chapter 2: The Table of Illumination: Journeying through Shadows	24
Journal Reflection: Journeying out of the Shadows	31
Chapter 3: The Table of Revelation: Embracing Authenticity	36
Journal Reflection: Embracing Authenticity	43
Chapter 4: The Table of Authority: Reclaiming Your Voice	49
Journal Reflection: Reclaiming Your Voice	59
Chapter 5: The Table of Serenity: Finding Stillness Within	64
Journal Reflection: Trading Worry for Rest in God	73
Chapter 6: The Table of Clarity: Deciphering Your Purpose	81
Journal Reflection: Embracing Your Identity and Purpose	88
Chapter 7: The Table of Redemption: Healing the Past and Embracing the Present	95
Journal Reflection: Healing the Past and Embracing the Present	107
Epilogue: Reflections and Steps on Your Journey to Healing	111
Journal Reflection: Beyond These Pages	115
Scripture to Meditate Upon	119
Bonus Chapter: Writing Your Own Story of Healing and Redemption	122

In the shadows of our past, we often find the light of our future. This is the essence of healing, the journey of rediscovery, and the profound grace of God's love. Join me as we unveil the table of our stories, where pain transforms into purpose, and brokenness is mended by faith.

BEFORE YOU BEGIN

This book is a call for those who have stood at a distance for far too long, burying their pain deep within until the scar over their hearts becomes numb. It is a call for the broken, the battered, and the weary—those ready to lay down the heavy loads they've carried.

This call reaches out to the captive, the broken-hearted, and the lost souls wandering in unfamiliar places. It is a call for you—a call to come. Come to the table.

Identity is the very core of who or what a person or thing is. From the very beginning, even before your memory took hold, you had an identity bestowed upon you from Heaven. His Word declares that, before you were formed, you were known.

God knit you together in your mother's womb. You were always his, from the start (Jeremiah 1:5, Psalm 139:13). Somewhere along the way, you may have forgotten, and that's okay. We all experience moments of forgetfulness.

What matters now, at this moment, is that you begin recognizing the voices that made you forget—voices that whispered lies about your true identity and voices that tried to redefine who you are.

But fear not, my sweet sister. Through the pages of this book, I hope you will remember. I hope you find peace with the pain of the past and discover your purpose in the present.

> *"She remembered who she was, and the game changed."*
> —Unknown

I hope you will remember who you are and whom you truly belong to while reading this book, and I hope that everything changes for the good.

This book is written from the perspective that you've already given your life to Jesus. It is for the woman of God who feels held back, who is not fully living, who is hiding and not showing up due to past or present circumstances.

However, if you've picked up this book by chance and are not a child of God, I want you to know that this book is for you too. Throughout its pages and stories, I hope you find yourself.

Whether you have accepted Jesus as your Savior and know you are God's child, or you haven't realized it yet, my prayer is that, by the time you finish reading, you will have a new understanding of yourself—who you were always meant to be, who you are right now, who you are becoming, and where you truly belong.

I pray that you will come to know and fully believe that God's table is a place where you don't have to fight for belonging. It's not about being the "pretty" girl or the "popular" girl. You don't even have to have it all figured out. You can come as you are, exactly how you are right now, to His table. A seat is waiting just for you.

Dear friend, do you know that the greatest power you have over the enemy is when you decide to let the truth come out? There is so much power in letting the truth—the truth of what happened to you, the truth of the words spoken over you, the truth of your mistakes, the truth of your true identity, and the truth of your story—to the surface.

I believe that now, more than ever, it's your time. It's your time to bring the dark areas into the light once and for all. It's time to share that light with the world. I want to encourage you to be open and honest with God throughout this process.

When you rise up, despite everything the enemy has put in your path to destroy you, and you embrace God's plan and calling for your life, you are looking the enemy straight in the eye and putting him in his place.

As you read these words, you may feel many things rising to the surface—pain, hurt, memories, mistakes, rejection—things you thought were long gone. But you'll realize that you had merely covered them up, hiding them beneath a thin layer of dirt and a pretty smile. I know this because I too for far too long buried things way down, but as I decided to allow the truth to rise to the surface, I was able to bring the darkness to light and healing began. I knew that I had to do this for myself, for others, for you and for generations to come.

As you allow your story to rise, as you soak in the words of truth, as you let the truth come out regardless of what it looks like for you, things will shift. You will finally begin to embrace the true power over the enemy. Your healing too will begin.

No longer will he keep you at tables where you don't belong. No longer will he steal your joy and peace. No longer will he prevent you from taking your rightful seat at the table where you've always belonged. No longer will you walk in false identities or conceal your pain.

Sister, I am praying for you as you read each chapter, as you write your story alongside me, and as you process the pain. I can picture us sitting together at my kitchen table, sipping warm coffee as I reach across and hold your hand. I wish as we begin this deep healing work, learning how to let forgiveness reign, how to find peace with the past, surrender it all to our Heavenly Father and begin to see the purpose of the pain for us today, that I could just give you a big hug. Even though I can't hug you right now, know that I am praying for you. A hug is only temporary anyways, and this prayer I'm praying for you is eternal. I'm praying that you'll have divine revelations, moments of complete surrender, overwhelming feelings of resting in his love and open arms. I'm praying that you begin to find healing, know that you can use all that the enemy has hurled at you and create a purpose that will become your legacy.

As you begin, I want you to know that this journey to finding yourself; shedding the labels the world has placed upon you; and overcoming fatherlessness, brokenness, and feelings of being unloved will not be easy. Forgive me for sounding cliché, but it will be worth it. At times, you'll feel like you're taking steps backwards, but rest assured as you place the bow and arrow of your life in Heavenly Father's hands, the tension and pressure will accelerate to its intended target. Your pain, your past, your story in God's hands is just being pulled back to be in position for your greatest purpose yet. Soon, you'll see that glimmer of light in the darkness. You'll see the table and the chair that has been waiting for you all along.

I understand how difficult it is to write your story, to let your truth out. It has taken me years, and it may take you just as long. Honestly, the story you'll read within these pages is not even half of my story. There were some parts that were just for me and other parts that no matter how difficult it was for me had to be told. I'm sure as you journey through your story too, you'll find the same is true. But then, one day or night, you'll awaken and realize it's all pouring out—the lost and stolen parts of yourself are being recovered. You're finding healing in the process, and your power is returning.

My advice? Embrace every step. Take your time. Give yourself grace. Read a chapter, put it down, and come back to it. Write without overthinking. Just respond however your heart tells you to. Tell it all to Jesus, even if you never tell it to anyone else. Just the process of letting it out will be a step towards your healing and your purpose.

I found it easier to tell my story through different means. I wanted none of it to be fiction because there is an anointing in the true story. So, know that, even though names might not be revealed in the beginning, the stories are true. Every word happened. I had to write it that way to process through it and to reinforce to myself that I am no longer that person. I am a victor. I have placed it all in his hands now and as you read it, the arrow is on its way to its intended target and purpose. To help you, to let you know that you're not alone. To let you know that you're going to make it. To let you know that healing can come, that you do have a place, a seat at the table.

I encourage you to write your pain out too, in whatever way feels right to you. Release it. Surrender it once and for all. God is here with us. He is in our story. I hope that what I share with you will bring you hope, freedom, healing, restoration, and the courage to bring all darkness into the fullness of light and in return you do the same for someone else.

The first part of my story is the hardest; thus, the first chapter is as well. However, I felt the need to write it out and share it with you so you can be brave enough to share your story too. It's okay to let it out, to release it, and to help someone else do the same. My intention in sharing my journey is that someone else will know and believe in the goodness of God despite it all, that you too can say, "I will make it through." I hope within these pages we begin to see a need for doors to open to conversations that have needed to happen for far too long, that you will begin to find that you're not alone and it's okay to not be okay, but it's not meant for us to stay that way.

Are you ready, friend? Are you ready to learn how to rip off the labels imposed by the world, your pain, and your past mistakes? Are you ready to discover who you truly are and where you genuinely belong? Go through this book with deep prayer, love, a cup of something warm, and a pencil to journal your story and your thoughts.

Let's embark on our journey to His table.

Throughout our lives, often without realizing it, we find ourselves seated at countless tables. We gather around tables to share meals with our families, solve problems, write, work, learn, entertain, be entertained, build relationships, fellowship, draw, talk, listen, wait, play games, be nourished, and sometimes simply to rest.

As we undertake this journey, we will realize that some tables where we've sat were never intended for us. Some we've tried to fit into but never felt right. Then there is the one—the one table where, when you finally arrive, you just know. It is the table, His table, where you belonged all along. A seat is waiting there for you that, unlike a fairy tale, is designed to fit you just right.

Disclaimer: I am not a licensed therapist or counselor. This book may contain content that could be triggering for individuals who have experienced trauma. If you require assistance in these areas, please reach out to a professional for support and guidance.

She remembered who she was,
and the game changed.

CHAPTER 1

The Table of Unveiling:
Bringing Darkness to the Light

She scampered barefoot, her tiny feet moving as swiftly as they could across the rough path littered with thorny bushes. It was a scorching summer day, and tears blurred her vision and streamed down her face, mixing with beads of sweat. Her little heart felt as if it would shatter into a million pieces, making it hard to breathe.

Tully caught a glimpse of her mother standing at the gate in the distance, but she didn't seek comfort there. All she wanted was to pass through that gate, run back to the house, and hide in the safety of the closet, even if just for a little while.

As she neared the gate, Tully heard her mother's voice asking what they had done. Her mother tried to grasp her arm to halt her escape, but Tully refused to stop. She had to keep running, knowing that if she paused to explain, the pain would only intensify.

Without hesitating, Tully dashed into the house, slowing down only when she was inside. Her heart still raced, but her footsteps grew quieter. In the hallway, she heard heavy snoring, indicating the presence of the "big bad man" she feared.

Carefully tiptoeing, she crept past him and sought refuge in the back of the closet—the place where she felt the most hidden and secure. She knew no one would enter the "big bad man's" room to find her. They were all too afraid. Tully was scared, too, but she had learned that it was the one place where she could escape their notice and feel safe, if only for a little while.

Curling up in the farthest corner of the closet, Tully attempted to push the day's events from her mind. However, the memories persisted, refusing to fade. Earlier that day, a new cousin had arrived, raising her hopes of finding companionship and safety. The other children in the house had invited her to play in the barn. Tully, accustomed to being left alone, had eagerly joined them, hoping that the presence of the new cousin would shield her from harm. But her hopes were shattered.

Everything happened so quickly—she found herself thrown to the ground while the other children watched. An older boy pressed himself onto her. Though she didn't understand what was happening, she felt an overwhelming sense of dirtiness and shame. The laughter of the other children echoed in her ears. Before she could get up, an older girl wielded a pair of scissors, warning Tully of dire consequences if she dared to speak out.

As Tully lay there in the closet, she couldn't fathom how anyone could hurt her more than what she had already experienced. All she wanted was to forget that this day had ever happened. With the cold seeping into the closet, she huddled into a ball, finding solace beneath a large coat.

When Tully awoke, darkness enveloped her. The absence of the familiar snoring indicated that the "big bad man" had left, if only for a while. Her entire body ached. Her legs trembled, and even her lips felt numb. Tully's stomach growled, reminding her of her hunger. Slowly, she emerged from the closet, her steps cautious and quiet. She headed to the kitchen, avoiding the refrigerator to prevent any noise that might disturb others.

Her mother was nowhere to be seen, but her presence or absence hardly made a difference—Tully never felt safe when she was around. The other children were gone, too, and she wondered if anyone had even noticed or cared where she disappeared to when she sought refuge. There were no calls from her mother, and no one was looking for her.

The table stood before her, a chilling reminder of loneliness. Dirty bowls, leftover food, and empty beer cans littered its surface. Tully dreaded drinking from any cup or can that was left unattended on that table. She had witnessed one of the older boys urinating into them and tricking others into consuming it. The smallest and most defenseless, Tully feared becoming their next target for cruel pranks.

She vividly recalled the day when the men lounged in the living room, smoking and laughing, barely able to move. They conspired, suggesting it would be amusing if Tully joined them in smoking. One of them brought the burning white stick to her lips, urging her to take a puff while they all laughed. The sickness that followed lingered for hours, and Tully vowed to steer clear of their presence whenever they gathered.

On the table, Tully discovered a bowl of leftover butter beans and a small glass of water. She knew she needed to eat and clean herself up before daylight revealed her whereabouts. Taking the bowl and drink, she retreated to the bathroom—a place where others rarely bothered her, and the door had a lock.

She sat behind that locked door, her head pounding, her ears ringing. Weariness settled upon her small frame. The sound of a car door slamming announced her mother's return and prompted Tully to switch off the light, crawl into bed, and pretend to be asleep when her mother entered. She didn't have a bed of her own, but at least Tully felt a fleeting sense of companionship when her mother climbed into bed, even if it often went unnoticed.

The following day, Tully waited until the bus carrying the older children departed. She yearned to bury the painful memories of the previous day and sought solace in the presence of her beloved Barbie dolls—the cherished gifts her mother occasionally bought for her, as if they were tokens of reconciliation between them. Perhaps if she immersed herself in play, the day would pass by unnoticed, and everyone would leave her in peace. Tully often wondered if her days would ever be any different.

* * *

The bright morning sun beamed through a tiny crevice in the wall, casting its piercing light into the dark room where Mary lay. The room was filled with shattered pieces all around her, the smell of dirt and filth burned her nose. Her knees were drawn to her chest, her head buried between them, and she shivered as pain shook her body to the core. Tears continued to stream down her face, even though the ordeal was over.

Even though she tried with all her might, her body and mind refused to find stillness; the torment seemed endless. The only few minutes of solace that she could find was trying to recall the days when her Papa was alive, and she had to fight hard to suppress the memories of the previous night. This seemed to be her daily pattern now, pain and torment, darkness, filth, then a little glimmer of light, a few seconds of solace in better memories, only to have it start and end again the same way. She longed for her Papa's arms, his voice, a return to the days before, she yearned to go back and recapture her lost innocence—before the relentless torment, before the terrible mistakes that haunted her every thought. Every day, it seemed as if her Papa's voice was slipping away from her, his face becoming a distant memory. She felt herself fading, forgetting who she was before all of this. She could barely remember the girl she used to be.

Mary couldn't bear to face another day in the light. Hope had deserted her. She believed there was no one left to love her, no place to call her own, no sense of belonging. She believed she would never find those things again. In a whisper, just before her exhausted body succumbed to sleep, she pleaded, "God, help me." She knew only God, the true living God, could rescue her. Her Papa had taught her that, but now she felt too far gone, abandoned even by the so-called religious men, unworthy, ashamed, in a relentless cycle with no way out.

When darkness fell that night, Mary raised her still tired, sore body and mustered the courage to creep out the door. She had no destination in mind, only a desperate need to escape the house before another man arrived. Not tonight, tonight she just needed a few hours of something different, a few hours to imagine that things were different for her, a few hours to try and hear her Papa's voice and remember. She just wanted to find one glimpse of hope, surely somewhere out there walking alone she could find just a few moments of solace. Carefully concealing herself, she kept her head down, staring at her sore, dirty bare feet as she walked. The moon was brightly beaming down, and she found herself drifting farther and farther away. Maybe tonight she could have a different ending, maybe if she just said goodbye to this world on her own terms. The voices in her head and mind were so loud now, she knew she couldn't find any peace ever again, even out here all alone she was still tormented. As she walked alone considering her path, it was like she was being pulled by something now that was guiding her somewhere, to something and she continued on.

The moon, bright and beautiful, provided just enough light to illuminate her path. She had made her decision that she just couldn't live like this anymore. Somehow, someway tonight. It had to end. All of a sudden she heard something in the distance, with her eyes still down, she knew it was probably man and she was afraid that her plans would have to wait, maybe if she kept her head down the man would just leave her alone and let her go her way. But as she got closer, her head seemed to lift up on its own, and her gaze met his. That's when she first saw him—a man who seemed strangely familiar. The voices in her head seemed to intensify and yet at the same time she could feel peace. Unsure of what was happening, this internal struggle raging within, she just stopped and dropped to her knees. The man approached her slowly and called her by name. No one had done that for a very long time. At the sound of her name, she looked up once again and locked her eyes with his. There was something different about him, unlike the men she had encountered before. Despite the fear and panic that stirred within her, she sat there frozen trying to grasp this sense of peace and love that was overwhelming her heart. She had been right before, this night it would all end. That night changed everything. Mary would never be the same again. With one word, he had calmed it all. The voices that had held her in bondage for so long, the guilt, the shame, the life seemed to cease in just a few moments of time. No longer held captive, she would follow that man and serve him until her dying day. It was Jesus, the Messiah, the one who had come. He had restored her hope, reminding her of who she truly was. She was Mary, God's beloved daughter—loved, treasured, remembered, not forgotten. Mary was cleansed and made whole. It would take time for her to fully grasp it all, but at that moment, she was finally free.

In Luke 8:1-2 we read of Mary Magdalene. A woman with seven demons who was set free by an encounter with Jesus. I'm not sure how her story really went in real life, but I have a feeling it went something like what I wrote above. Without a doubt, we know that Mary was in so much pain and that one encounter with Jesus changed it all. Sister friend, one encounter with Jesus can change it all for you too. He can make the pain of the past stop, but we must be willing to let go and let him.

*   *   *

I often wonder how many other Tullys and Marys are out there. It pains me deeply to think of the emotional hurt and physical pain that human beings inflict upon one another when they are controlled by the enemy. It hurts even more when we inflict pain upon ourselves.

Oh, how the Father's heart must yearn for the day when he will tell Jesus to come and take his children home. No more pain, no more sorrow, no more temptations—every tear will be wiped away. Just one encounter with Jesus can remind us of who we are. Just one moment of truth from his Word can bring comfort and healing when we need it most.

My hope is that all the Tullys and Marys out there will find Jesus and that they will discover who they have always been. That is my purpose and mission in writing this book—to help you and others remember who you are and know that you are not defined by what happened. You are not defined by the mistakes you've made or by what the world says about you. You are God's daughter, my friend. Maybe you "know" that but aren't fully trusting, believing, and walking in it just yet. My hope is that soon you will be.

I wish I could say that things got easier for Tully, that she was rescued from her life of pain after that day, but the reality is different. Tully endured a lot of heartaches, as you will discover in this book. More abuse and hardships awaited her, leaving her wrestling with her identity for years to come.

Perhaps you are not a Tully, but something did happen to you. It might have occurred during your school years. It may have involved people you thought were friends but turned out to be otherwise. It might have happened in your adult life.

I remember sitting at a table with ten women once, and three of them admitted to being abused or witnessing abuse in their homes. Given more time, that number would likely have grown. The truth is, you have probably sat at a table recently with women who have experienced abuse or some form of hurt.

Maybe you were that woman, and chances are you never shared your pain with anyone. Perhaps you confided in someone only to be made to feel that it was a lie, that it never happened. Maybe you even convinced yourself that it wasn't a big deal. But if it weighs on your heart and mind, then it is significant. Even if it's just taking the time to write your truth, that's a step forward.

Abuse can take different forms—physical, verbal, or even the aftermath of a traumatic accident. Reflect on a time in your life when you began to shrink back, when you started to change. What was it that made you retreat? It was that moment when the enemy started to steal your voice.

Together, let us declare today that we will no longer allow what happened to us to steal from us. We will find our voices again and reclaim our true identities in Him. Remember, you are not alone in this. God is there with you, and I am praying for you.

We have all sat at various tables where pain engulfed us, with each experience being unique. We have sat with women who concealed their pain for far too long, burying it deep within, allowing it to harden their hearts and define their worth with labels that were never meant to stick.

With his cunning ways, the enemy wants to keep you trapped in your hurt. He whispers that it's too scary to let it out, that it won't do any good after all this time. He tries to convince you that it happened for a reason, making you question God's goodness. I wrestled with those lies for a long time until the truth came and set me free. You see, God never intended for things to be this way.

In the beginning, God created a perfect, safe place for his children—the Garden of Eden. Suffering, pain, and evil were never part of His plan. But Lucifer, a beautiful angel, desired to be God and deceived Adam and Eve in the garden. Since then, we have been born into a fallen world, a world of sin ruled by the prince of darkness.

But God made another plan to restore us one day to that perfect place. While we journey through this earthly life, our purpose is to recognize the power we have over the enemy by not letting his plans prevail. Every time we confront the truth, his tactics, and his strategies, we reclaim our power. We declare that we will live despite it all. We will tell others that this world is not our home and that our pain, past, and mistakes do not define us.

When I think of Tully's life, I'm reminded of Mary Magdalene. I wonder how much pain Mary had to endure to be possessed by seven demons. It's easy to become controlled by our past pain and mistakes when we bury or numb ourselves with anything other than the truth. Mary Magdalene had allowed her past pain and mistakes to possess her in a literal sense. But Mary was delivered, and from then on, she devoted herself to Jesus, allowing His true light to diminish all the hurt, pain, and darkness.

If you have never given your life to Jesus, now is the time. Let go of the past, and don't let it bind you any longer. You can learn to trust God again and let His light overcome the darkness. You no longer have to sit alone at cold, dark, and scary tables. You are not that person anymore. You are not defined by what happened to you. You have a voice, a story to tell, and a purpose. You belong somewhere and to someone. You are more precious than any jewel or treasure on this earth.

Remember that what happened to you is not who you are. Your identity is separate from the bad things that happened to you. It's crucial to bring your experiences out of the darkness into the light, to peel apart the pain from your true self. Take a deep breath and release the pain. Inhale the truth, envision the sun's warmth surrounding you, and know that it's time to start sitting at a new table.

Let us rewrite our story together into one of healing, strength, and restoration.

JOURNAL REFLECTION
Finding Healing and Restoration

Today, as you reflect on the powerful journey we have explored in this chapter, dive deeper into your own experiences, pain, and hope for healing and restoration. Allow your heart and mind to be open to the transformative work of God in your life as you follow these journal prompts and meditate on the scriptures.

Reflection

Reflect on your own journey. Take a moment to recall times in your life when you have felt trapped, burdened, or silenced by past hurts or experiences.

Journal Prompts

Write down any memories or emotions that come to mind. Allow yourself to acknowledge the pain and the longing for healing. _____

_____
_____
_____
_____
_____
_____
_____
_____
_____
_____

"The Lord is nigh unto them that are of a broken heart; and saveth such as be of a contrite spirit." (Psalm 34:18 KJV)

Come to the Table

Surrender to God. Consider the importance of surrendering your pain and brokenness to God. Reflect on the significance of releasing the burden and allowing God to work in your life. Write a prayer expressing your willingness to surrender and trust in His healing power. _____

_____
_____
_____
_____
_____
_____
_____
_____
_____
_____
_____
_____
_____
_____
_____
_____
_____
_____
_____
_____
_____
_____
_____

"Come unto me, all ye that labour and are heavy laden, and I will give you rest." (Matthew 11:28 KJV)

Come to the Table

Embrace your true identity. Contemplate the truth that your past does not define you. Reflect on the unique identity and purpose that God has for you. Write down affirmations of your true identity in Him and the hopes and dreams you have for your future. _____
_____
_____
_____
_____
_____
_____
_____

"But ye are a chosen generation, a royal priesthood, an holy nation, a peculiar people; that ye should shew forth the praises of him who hath called you out of darkness into his marvellous light." (1 Peter 2:9 KJV)

Seek healing and restoration. Consider the steps you can take toward healing and restoration. Reflect on the importance of seeking support from others, embracing vulnerability, and allowing God's grace to transform your pain into a testimony. Write down practical steps you can take on your journey toward healing. _____
_____
_____
_____
_____
_____
_____
_____

"He healeth the broken in heart, and bindeth up their wounds." (Psalm 147:3 KJV)

Pray for others. Extend your reflections to include those around you who may be silently carrying their own burdens. Pray for their healing, restoration, and courage to seek help and embrace their true identity in Christ. _____

_____
_____
_____
_____
_____
_____
_____
_____
_____
_____
_____
_____
_____
_____
_____
_____
_____

"Bear ye one another's burdens, and so fulfill the law of Christ."
(Galatians 6:2 KJV)

Remember, journaling is a sacred space for self-reflection and a conversation with God. Allow yourself the freedom to pour out your heart, express your thoughts and emotions honestly, and receive His love, healing, and restoration as you embark on this transformative journey.

Prayer

Dear Heavenly Father,

As I embark on this journey of healing and self-discovery, I come before You with an open heart and a willingness to face the pain of my past. You know the depths of my soul, and I trust that You are with me every step of the way.

Lord, help me to remember that I am fearfully and wonderfully made by Your loving hands. In moments of doubt, remind me that I am Your masterpiece, created for a purpose beyond my understanding.

I acknowledge the times when I've allowed past hurts and mistakes to hold me back, to cast shadows on my identity and purpose. Please reveal to me Your perspective on these situations, that I may find freedom in Your truth.

In the words of 2 Corinthians 12:9a, "My grace is sufficient for you, for my power is made perfect in weakness." Lord, I surrender my weaknesses, my pain, and my brokenness to You. May Your grace and strength be my guide on this journey.

Help me to identify any false tables in my life where I've sought validation from the wrong sources or allowed labels to define me. Grant me the wisdom to discern the tables that align with Your truth and purpose for my life.

As I reflect on my unhealed pain and trauma, I ask for Your healing touch, Lord. Show me how these experiences have shaped me and how they may have hindered me from fully embracing the abundant life You have prepared for me.

Guide me in bringing my pain and trauma to Your table of healing and restoration. I surrender it to You, knowing that Your love is the ultimate source of healing.

Thank You, Lord, for calling me Your daughter and for the promise of a new identity in You. I embrace this truth and the impact it has on my life and purpose.

In Jesus' name, I pray. Amen.

Oh, our precious Jesus, our Savior and friend. He meets us right where we are, amidst our brokenness, tragedy, pain, and mistakes. He simply shows up and loves us.

CHAPTER 2

The Table of Illumination: Journeying through Shadows

Sitting at the small, cozy table with a kind older woman and a few other girls her age, Tully felt a sense of safety and happiness, even though she didn't fully understand what was happening. She found it difficult to focus on the people around her because everything in the room seemed so beautiful.

The wooden floor, the walls, the music, and the sunlight streaming through the window captivated her. She kept her head down but observed her surroundings, taking it all in. Having experienced cruelty from most children she knew, Tully was content not to engage in idle chatter. She yearned for a break from the meanness that had permeated her life.

When the woman opened a big book filled with words, Tully's eyes were immediately drawn to the picture on the wall behind her. It portrayed a man she had never seen before, but based on what she had heard throughout the week, she believed it was Jesus.

As the teacher read, an indescribable warmth washed over Tully, unlike anything she had ever felt. It was as if she were lying outside on a pleasant summer day with the sun's warm rays beating down on her face, filling her heart with joy. Calmness, brightness, and love enveloped her. Tully listened intently as the teacher described the Holy Spirit descending on Jesus like a dove during his baptism (Luke... 3:22).

Upon hearing those words while gazing at the picture, she knew that Jesus was her friend. He had been the one to help her, and for the rest of her life, he would be her refuge.

Tully's thoughts drifted back to that frightful day when the police arrived and her cousins told her to hide. Similar situations had occurred before when they had put things in her pants at the store and made her run home with them. However, this time was different. Something ominous was happening, and she felt that it was all connected to her.

When her mother called for her, Tully's fears were confirmed. As they both sat in the back of the police car with a man, her mother was crying uncontrollably and clutching her tightly. Where were they going? Why was her mother crying so intensely and holding on so tightly? Tully was gripped by terror, with no inkling of what awaited her.

A few minutes later, they arrived at their destination, and the man forcefully took Tully from her mother's arms. Hearing her mother's cries, Tully felt so frightened that breathing became a struggle. The man hurriedly led Tully through a building and out another door, where she spotted some familiar faces.

Just a few weeks earlier, while shopping at the local Walmart with her mom, they had encountered these people. They had seemed kind and strangely familiar and were delighted to see Tully. They came for a few visits, bearing gifts and sharing in the Christmas spirit. Although Tully didn't fully grasp the concept of Christmas, these individuals were gentle, shedding tears when they departed.

Now, here she was with those familiar faces, being placed in the back of their car. Fear consumed her as the car sped away, driving for what seemed like hours and hours into the vast unknown. Despite her mother's shortcomings as a parent and Tully's constant sense of insecurity, her mother had provided moments of respite, making her feel less alone in the world. But now, she was gone.

Finally, when they reached their destination, Tully noticed an overwhelming sense of joy from the people who eagerly greeted her. They showered her with hugs. Before she knew it, she found herself seated at a new table. This table was different. It emanated warmth and abundance with an array of food and smiling faces surrounding her. She would soon discover that this was her family—her dad, aunts, and grandmother.

Tully reflected on this while the teacher continued reading, and she began to believe that Jesus had played a role in bringing her here. It was the first time that she truly felt free from the dark, cold closet where she had spent most of her time. Now, she basked in the light, the warmth, and a sense of safety.

As Tully grew, her mother gradually stopped coming around. Many times throughout her life, she encountered Jesus just when she needed him most.

*   *   *

Once we acknowledge our pain, surrender it to God, and embark on the journey of healing, there are moments when we must encounter God or remember the encounters we have had with him. Take a moment now to pause and reflect. When did you first hear about Jesus? Turn to the journal section at the end of the chapter and write about that moment. What do you remember about it? Did you surrender your life to him then, or did you simply feel his presence? Do you recall a sensation of light, love, or warmth? How did he reveal himself to you at that moment?

Oh, our precious Jesus, our Savior and friend. He meets us right where we are, amidst our brokenness, tragedy, pain, and mistakes. He simply shows up and loves us.

When I think of Tully's first encounter with Jesus, it reminds me of a day when God spoke to me so profoundly that it shook me to my core. It appeared to be an ordinary day, but I've come to realize that God uses those seemingly ordinary days to teach us extraordinary lessons. I was caught up in the busyness of work, rushing from one place to another with a lengthy to-do list that seemed impossible to complete within the remaining hours of the day. Dressed in my work attire, including heels, I headed toward the downtown area of our town, parked my car, and set out on foot.

The summer day was sweltering with thick, humid air. As I stepped out of my car, I heard the distant rumble of thunder. An office visit was my first stop, and I quickly inquired about directions to my next destination. I chose to ignore the lady's advice to retrieve my umbrella from my car. After all, a busy woman in heels doesn't like to backtrack when there's so much to accomplish.

As I hurriedly proceeded to my next stop, the thunder grew louder, and the once-bright sky turned dark. Deep down, I whispered a plea to God, hoping to make it back to my car before the storm unleashed its fury.

Running uphill in painful heels, anxiety creeping in, I opened the car door just as the first raindrops began to fall. Shutting the door, I found myself in the midst of a deluge. Rain poured down so heavily that visibility was severely impaired. It became evident that my plans for the day had been derailed—I was done, and my to-do list would have to wait.

As I focused on navigating through the rain-soaked streets, my attention was unexpectedly drawn to the rearview mirror. There, in the downpour, I saw the outline of a woman struggling against the storm.

Questions flooded my mind. Why is she walking in this relentless downpour? Concerned, I heard God's voice, clear and resolute, instructing me to go back and offer her a ride. I hesitated, wrestling with my own hesitations and excuses. The rain was torrential, she was already soaked, and I needed to find shelter for myself. What if she posed a threat?

Nevertheless, I relented, acknowledging that I would heed God's request. I made a U-turn, intending to locate the woman and provide her with respite from the rain. But as I circled the area, searching, my heart sank. She was nowhere to be found.

Regret washed over me. Why hadn't I acted promptly when God first asked me to help her? I hoped that someone else had offered her assistance or that she had found refuge elsewhere. However, a realization hit me, and tears welled in my eyes. Why did God prompt me to go back for her if she wouldn't be there? What purpose did it serve?

Then came the answer that pierced my heart. "I rescued you so you could rescue her." Even now, years later, as I pen these words, the memory brings tears to my eyes. Just as Tully had been rescued from darkness, her life forever altered, my own rescue had taken place when someone prayed for me, and Jesus showed up. That's why she recognized the light so readily. You see, when people find themselves in a dark room, they are immediately drawn to the first glimmer of light they see.

Dear friend, you, too, have been rescued from darkness. At some point in life, something happened—a hurt, a loss, a mistake, or a betrayal. It may still cause you pain, but the moment you whispered the name of Jesus, you were rescued from that darkness. Darkness cannot dwell where there is light; light always overcomes the dark. God chose that ordinary day to remind me that I was not walking in my purpose and calling at that time in my life. He revealed that I had been rescued to rescue others as well.

I may never know if the woman truly existed or if she was a divine encounter orchestrated by God. However, the lesson remains etched in my soul—I must not miss my assignments in life. Despite my human frailty and the missed opportunities that may arise, I will always remember that I have been rescued to rescue.

That's precisely why you are reading this book now, in this season of your life—to remind you that you are not alone, that you belong at His table.

There was a time in my life when I sat at a table of darkness, but Jesus brought me to His table of light. Sometimes, circumstances led me to tables of darkness that I didn't choose. Other times, my own decisions led me astray. Past pain, failures, mistakes, and the hurtful words of others occasionally kept me from sitting at the table with Jesus.

Yet, through surrendering it all to Him and continually running to Him, I discovered healing at Jesus' table. It is a place of forgiveness, safety, peace, and joy. Oh, my friend, I am grateful that His invitation was open to me and that it extends to every person I know.

Will you open yourself to His transformative power? Will you surrender all, allowing Him to shape your life and guide your steps? Are you ready to give Him everything?

Today marks the beginning of a profound journey—a journey of surrender, growth, and transformation. It won't happen overnight. It will require time and effort. But fear not, for you will be equipped with an abundance of grace, both from within and bestowed upon you by Him. His storehouse overflows with the grace, mercy, and love necessary to fuel your every step on this path.

Never forget that you possess a unique purpose in this vast tapestry of existence. Your calling beckons you, urging you to take your place at a different table. It's time to leave behind the shadows of the past and embrace the brilliance of your divine destiny. Embracing this new chapter allows you to step into your full potential and become a guiding light for others.

So, my friend, will you allow Him to work in your life, shaping and refining you? Will you surrender your fears, doubts, and limitations, opening yourself to the infinite possibilities that await?

It all begins with a single choice—a choice to yield to His plan and purpose for your life.

Today, you stand on the precipice of transformation. Embrace the journey ahead, knowing that you are not alone. Draw from His overflowing storehouse of grace and venture forth with confidence. You have a purpose to fulfill, a calling to embrace. It is time to take your seat at the table where your truest self awaits.

May your surrender lead to freedom, your growth inspire others, and your journey ignite a flame of hope. This is your time to shine. Let the chapters of your life unfold with courage and grace.

JOURNAL REFLECTION
Journeying out of the Shadows

"For ye were sometimes darkness, but now are ye light in the Lord: walk as children of light." (Ephesians 5:8 KJV)

Reflection

Today, as I reflect on Tully's encounter with Jesus and the transformative power of His love, I am reminded of my own journey. Just as Tully experienced a shift from darkness to light, I have been rescued and brought into the embrace of God's glorious light.

Scripture tells us that we were once dwelling in darkness, lost and without hope. But through Christ, we have been given a new identity as children of light. We have been called to live in the radiance of His truth, love, and grace.

Thinking back to that significant moment when I first encountered Jesus, I recall the overwhelming warmth, love, and peace that flooded my heart. It was as if a veil was lifted, and I found myself basking in the glorious presence of the Almighty. In that encounter, I realized that Jesus was not only my Savior but also my ever-present friend, offering solace and guidance through life's challenges.

Today, I am reminded that my journey with Jesus is not a solitary one. He has called me to be a beacon of His light, extending His love and compassion to those around me. Just as I have been rescued, I am called to be an instrument of rescue for others.

Scripture encourages us to live as children of light, to let His light shine through us in all that we do. It is through our actions, words, and attitudes that we have the opportunity to bring hope, healing, and the love of Christ to a world longing for transformation.

Journal Prompts

Reflect on your own encounter with Jesus and write down the details of that transformative moment. _____

_____
_____
_____
_____
_____
_____
_____
_____
_____
_____
_____
_____

Consider the ways in which Jesus has rescued you from darkness. How has His love and grace brought light into your life? _____

_____
_____
_____
_____
_____
_____
_____
_____
_____
_____
_____
_____
_____

Meditate on Ephesians 5:8 and ponder what it means to live as a child of light. How can you actively reflect His light in your daily interactions and relationships? _____
_____
_____
_____
_____
_____
_____

Pray for guidance and strength to embrace your calling and be a source of light and hope to those around you. _____
_____
_____
_____
_____
_____
_____

Take a moment to thank God for His faithfulness and the privilege of being a part of His redemptive work in the world. _____
_____
_____
_____
_____
_____
_____

Prayer

Heavenly Father,

Thank You for rescuing me from darkness and bringing me into Your marvelous light. Help me to continually surrender to Your will and purpose for my life. Fill me with Your grace, that I may live as a true reflection of Your love and be a source of hope to those around me. Guide me on this journey, Lord, as I seek to embrace my calling and sit at the table of light.

In Jesus' name, I pray.

Amen.

Who she had been was not who she was.
What had happened to her did not define her.

CHAPTER 3

*The Table of Revelation:
Embracing Authenticity*

Tully's trembling form found solace within the confines of the bathroom stall. Tears cascaded down her flushed cheeks, carrying the weight of the pain she bore within. The transition to yet another school had been arduous. Tully fought hard to conceal her struggles, but she felt like an unwelcome burden to her already burdened family.

The cruel words of her peers only added to her shame, as they targeted her early development, subjecting her to unwanted attention and baseless rumors. The boys' lewd remarks haunted her, while the girls accused her of seeking attention by falsifying her appearance. Tully cared little for the opinions of others, though. All she yearned for was to be left alone and loved unconditionally.

As the whispers of her peers circulated, Tully also faced the painful truth of her unconventional family dynamics. When her classmates shared stories of their traditional households, Tully couldn't relate. The absence of her parents cast a shadow over her heart, causing her to question her own worthiness of their love.

The nickname "orphan Annie" pierced through her like a dagger. Meanwhile, she was left to grapple with the unknown reasons behind her parents' choices. Was she to blame for their absence? Was she somehow responsible for their lack of affection? Her longing for normal family dynamics and a sense of belonging left unanswered questions that unknowingly shaped her identity.

Upon returning to the classroom, Tully was met with a well-intentioned but flawed mantra from her teacher. "Sticks and stones can break your bones, but words can't hurt you." The words echoed hollowly in her wounded soul. The bruises on her spirit were invisible but deeply felt.

Tully couldn't escape the pain inflicted by the spoken and unspoken judgments she endured during those formative years. Slowly but surely, she began to lose sight of herself, her voice, and her rightful place at the table. Daily attendance at school became an obligatory chore, a mere existence she had to bear.

As time passed, Tully learned to navigate the complexities of her emotions, masking her pain and seeking solace in temporary distractions. She wore her beautiful smile as a shield, played her assigned roles with precision, and sought love in the wrong places. Desperate to conceal her brokenness, she struggled to let anyone see her real self—the fragmented parts she believed were unlovable.

Though she entrusted her pain to her friend Jesus, moments of imperfection and failure left her consumed by shame, guilt, and feelings of unworthiness. She attempted to fill the void with various pursuits, but nothing could heal the deep-seated wounds she carried. Violated once again by a man, her trust in others shattered, and body image issues drove her down the path of self-punishment through an eating disorder.

Behind the facade of a popular straight-A student, Tully's shattered pieces remained scattered and unhealed. All she longed for was to be loved unconditionally, to attain a semblance of perfection that would shield her from further harm. The burden of being a source of trouble to others weighed heavily on her weary soul, at times even leading her to contemplate the unimaginable.

Yet, another encounter with God was on the horizon, and it held the promise of change and restoration.

*   *   *

There's a woman in the Bible who had an encounter with Jesus, someone who, like Tully, had found herself sitting at tables where she didn't belong. I imagine that she had experienced her fair share of unwanted attention from men, perhaps from a young age.

While the Bible doesn't provide much information about her life before this encounter, I have known women like her—hopeless and broken—seeking solace in anything and everything that could fill the void within. I have been that woman.

According to the Bible, this woman had been married five times, and the man she was with at that moment was not even her husband. However, her story was about to take a different turn. We can only speculate about the circumstances that led her to that point—whether it was a series of unfortunate events or a chain of poor choices. Regardless, her encounter with Jesus was imminent. She was about to be called out of her darkness and into the light.

For so long, she had listened to the voices of others and lost sight of her own identity and what she truly needed. She found herself trapped in situations with no apparent way out.

The story goes that she arrived at the well during an unconventional hour, hoping to avoid encountering other women and their piercing glances. Their whispers and avoidance had become unbearable. She would never fit in, no matter how hard she tried.

On that particular day, she couldn't see a way forward. Hope seemed lost, and she longed to collect her water, retreat to her home, and abandon it all. Exhausted from living a lie, she strove to improve only to find herself trapped repeatedly in the same cycle.

Come to the Table

To her surprise, there was a man resting by the well when she arrived. Despite her initial impulse to turn away, she continued toward the well. After all, she needed water, and she didn't want to return later. As she approached, she noticed that the man at the well was a Jew—a relief, for he surely wouldn't engage in conversation with her. Yet, as she began to draw water, he spoke to her, and his words felt like a warm current running down her spine.

For the first time in her life, she felt seen, safe, and hopeful. He simply asked for a drink, but why would he ask her, someone with whom he should not even interact? Someone upon whom he should not even cast his eyes. She was grateful that he knew nothing about her.

But what he said next, as their eyes locked, would change her life forever. He revealed her past, revealed his own identity, and at that moment, as she chose to believe, her identity collided with his. That day, she arrived at the well, broken, lost, devoid of hope, enshrouded in lies, haunted by whispers. But she would depart forever changed.

Who she had been was not who she was. What had happened to her did not define her. She had spent her entire life searching, struggling to find this revelation. Now, in this moment, she felt it, and she knew she would never be the same. She no longer cared what others thought or how they spoke about her. She was transformed, and they would witness it. She had finally encountered the true light, love incarnate, and he introduced himself as Jesus.

* * *

That story moves me every time. I once witnessed it portrayed in a play, and being a visual person, I wept uncontrollably. When Jesus looked at her by the well, and she felt his presence enveloping her, she became overwhelmed with excitement. She left her water container and ran back to tell others.

Jesus sees you, my friend. He truly sees you, right in the middle of it all. I don't know what your current circumstances look like—maybe you're a mom surrounded by chaos with toddlers running amok. Maybe you're at the end of your parenting season facing an empty nest. Maybe your problem area is your marriage. Maybe it's choices you've made along the way, your finances, your career, that family dynamic, or church. Maybe you feel like you've lost yourself.

Can I share a secret with you? You haven't lost yourself; you're simply in a different season. The woman at the well was in a challenging season too.

Here's the good news: Jesus will meet you right there, precisely where you're hiding. In your loneliness, your pain, your grief, your moments of feeling inadequate, your mistakes, when it seems like nobody around you cares, when you're unsure of your identity, and at every table where you feel like you don't belong, He will be there.

He will meet you in your season. Right when you feel like giving up because all hope is lost, in the most unexpected moments, Jesus is there, ready to encounter you with His love and light.

The woman at the well, Tully, and countless others have grappled with identity issues throughout their lives. The enemy revels in this struggle. The voices we hear from others continually tempt us to compare ourselves to unrealistic standards, to flawless women in perfect worlds that don't exist.

We fail to recognize our true worth as members of the body of Christ. Jealousy, envy, comparison, doubt, inadequacy, shortcomings, shame, and guilt—they all become our daily companions. There have been moments when I allowed the actions of others, even my own, to define who I am. But we are not unworthy, not in the eyes of our Heavenly Father.

Our identity has always been and will always be that of His daughters. Yet the world will try to convince us otherwise. The pain, the mistakes, the heartaches, the hardships—these are mere whispers of the enemy to our souls. They tell us that we don't belong, that we are irreparably broken, that we've gone too far. The enemy's whispers sow doubt, make us forget, and deceive us into believing we can save ourselves or that we are undeserving of salvation. What labels have you allowed others to place upon you?

Even job titles, motherhood roles, marital statuses, church responsibilities, harsh words, or the weight of your past cannot define you. The pain and trauma you have endured do not dictate your identity. Let them out, and allow Him to begin the healing work within you today. You no longer have to sit at the table of an identity crisis.

Tully, much like the woman at the well and Mary Magdalene, carried the burden of an orphan spirit for most of her life—shackled by what had happened to her and the labels placed upon her. It would take her a considerable amount of time to unravel this truth. The orphan spirit takes hold of those who have experienced extreme rejection in life. It leads to patterns of isolation, comparison, false identity, fear-driven actions, and attempts to earn the love of others, even God's love.

Perhaps you recognize yourself in this struggle. Here's the good news: He is waiting at the well for you. Allow Him to begin the healing work within you today.

Today is the day to surrender it all to Him. He defines you. You are who He says you are—chosen, beautiful, and loved. Fearfully and wonderfully made. Sister, tear off all the labels today. Write them down and replace them with the truth. You are enough just as you are. Come to Him as you are today.

Take a moment to remember who you are, sister. Remember your true identity in Him and put an end to your identity crisis. You are His beloved, unconditionally. People may try to label you based on your actions, thinking they know it all, or you may carry secrets of which only you are aware. But these are not your identity. It's time to rediscover yourself and to embrace the truth of who you are. Nothing is more powerful than when a child of God realizes her true identity in Christ.

Declare today that the crisis is over. Join me in saying, "I remember who I am and to whom I belong. No longer will I believe the enemy's lies about who I am. No longer will I shrink back from my God-given purpose in this life. No longer will I pretend to be someone I am not." Today marks a new beginning. Embrace your true identity and walk confidently in the truth.

"Let the one who created you be the one who defines you." — Unknown

JOURNAL REFLECTION
Embracing Authenticity

Reflection

Take a moment to reflect on your journey through this chapter and the powerful message it holds about overcoming your identity crisis and finding your true identity in Christ. As you engage in this journal reflection, allow your thoughts and emotions to flow freely. Be open to the leading of the Holy Spirit. Write down your responses to the following prompts.

Journal Prompts

Describe a specific moment or aspect of the chapter that resonated with you deeply. Why do you think it impacted you so significantly?

_____
_____
_____
_____
_____
_____
_____
_____
_____
_____
_____

Come to the Table

Have you ever experienced an identity crisis or struggled with accepting your true identity as a child of God? How did this chapter help you gain a new perspective on your own journey? _____

_____
_____
_____
_____
_____
_____

Reflect on the labels or false identities that you have allowed others or even yourself to place upon you. Write down these labels and surrender them to God, inviting Him to replace them with His truth (e.g., "I am not worthy" becomes "I am chosen and loved"). _____

_____
_____
_____
_____
_____

Choose a scripture passage from the Bible that speaks to your heart regarding your identity in Christ. Write it down and reflect on its meaning for your life. Consider how this verse can help you combat the enemy's lies and reaffirm your true identity. _____

_____
_____
_____
_____
_____

How can you practically apply the lessons from this chapter to your life? Are there any specific actions or changes you feel prompted to make in order to align more fully with your true identity in Christ?

_____
_____
_____
_____
_____
_____
_____

As you ponder the following verse, consider what it means to be chosen, to be God's special possession. Reflect on the transformative power of stepping out of darkness and into the marvelous light of His love and truth. Let this scripture guide you in embracing your true identity and living it out with boldness and confidence.

> "But ye are a chosen generation, a royal priesthood, an holy nation, a peculiar people; that ye should shew forth the praises of him who hath called you out of darkness into his marvellous light:" (1 Peter 2:9, KJV)

_____
_____
_____
_____
_____
_____
_____
_____
_____
_____

Come to the Table

Take your time to pour out your heart onto these pages, allowing the words to serve as a conversation between you and God. Remember that He sees you, knows you intimately, and desires to reveal your true identity as His beloved child.

Prayer

Heavenly Father,

As I reflect on the labels and false identities that have clung to me, I come before You with an open heart. I acknowledge the weight they have placed upon my soul, the limitations they've imposed on my life, and the ways they've hindered me from fully embracing Your truth.

Lord, I surrender these burdensome labels to You. Take them from me, for I no longer wish to carry them. Replace the falsehoods with Your eternal truth. Transform my thinking, Lord, so that I may see myself as You see me – fearfully and wonderfully made, chosen, and deeply loved.

I cast aside "I am not worthy" and accept the gift of "I am chosen and loved" that You freely offer. Let Your truth resonate in the depths of my being, Lord, and guide my steps as I walk confidently in the identity You have bestowed upon me.

Thank You for Your grace and for rewriting my story with Your love and purpose. In Jesus' name, I pray.

Amen.

Let the one who created you
be the one who defines you.

CHAPTER 4

The Table of Authority: Reclaiming Your Voice

Sitting at her dressing table, Tully found herself lost in reflection as she delicately curled her long dark hair. The solitude enveloped her, and she gazed into the mirror, struggling to recognize the person staring back at her. In this moment of introspection, she sensed an overwhelming sense of loneliness, as if no one could truly comprehend the depth of pain she carried within. Tully longed to escape, to fade away from it all.

Life had dealt her numerous blows—reuniting with her estranged mother, yearning for family unity, preparing for her impending marriage—yet the nightmares, flashbacks, and resurfacing memories pushed her to her limits. It wasn't just the difficult teenage years, navigating her father's issues, or the recent toxic relationship she had escaped. Tully discovered that appearances could be deceiving, for behind the beautiful exterior lay darkness and torment. Recurring patterns of withdrawal, a coping mechanism from the past, seemed to ensnare her, threatening to shape her existence.

For far too long, Tully had been subjected to hurtful words, and she carried the burden of the hidden pain inflicted by her abusers. Now, revisiting the suppressed memories, she found herself teetering on the precipice of despair. As a mere spectator in her own life, survival became her primary goal. In this struggle, the beacon of light in her world was the one she loved, who was about to arrive to pick her up. With a sense of determination, Tully finished her preparations and stepped out into the world, oblivious to the rollercoaster of joy and hardship that awaited her in the coming years.

At the tender age of 17, Tully had ventured out on her own, shouldering the responsibilities of work and college. By 19, she was to marry her soulmate and bask in the happiness that marriage brought. However, her reunion with her mother proved fleeting and left her feeling abandoned once again.

As Tully embarked on her newlywed life, she soon discovered that the very thing she had longed for—a family of her own—was threatened. Faced with the cruel reality of an extreme case of endometriosis, she confronted the uncertainty of her ability to bear children. Sitting across from her doctor in that pivotal moment when she received the news, Tully felt her heart sink. She was unaware of the deep-seated generational trauma that wreaked havoc on her body, mind, and spirit. The physical ailment mirrored the emotional turmoil within. Could she ever experience the joy of motherhood?

A few days later, Tully had a life-changing encounter with Jesus, her friend, which set a course for the rest of her journey—a surrender so complete that it would reshape her existence. Kneeling before the altar, she offered her life to God, relinquishing the need to numb herself from the pain and longing. Her deepest desire was to be with her husband, have children, and serve God. The surrender marked a turning point.

A year later, Tully cradled her firstborn daughter in her hands, her husband having preached his first sermon the day before. The arrival of their child affirmed God's faithfulness. Another year brought the birth of their son, whose life began with a frightening ordeal as he stopped breathing at birth, necessitating an extended stay in the NICU. Yet, in the face of adversity, God once again proved His unwavering presence and love. Four years later, Tully's family was complete with the arrival of their third and final child, a baby girl. Despite the immense pain she had endured, Tully found solace and purpose in being a devoted wife and mother. Her love for her children knew no bounds.

Still, in the blessings, Tully grappled with feelings of unworthiness and struggled to find her place and voice in the world. Although she had embarked on a journey of placing God above all else in her life, the path to self-discovery and healing stretched before her. While Tully had come a long way, she knew there was more left to surrender and more wounds to be healed. The quest for her true purpose and to find her voice remained ongoing.

* * *

He sat at the table that night, his mind consumed with anxious thoughts. What could the King possibly want with someone like him? The weight of the moment compelled him to put his affairs in order, to bid farewell and express gratitude to those who had sustained him through the hardships of life. His dreams of a better future had long faded away. Perhaps he had never truly possessed hope.

Throughout his life, he had been confined to a state of dependence, crippled and reliant on others for his most basic needs. Once, he had been a grandson of the King, living in a grand palace filled with abundance. But the tragic day his father and grandfather passed away shattered his world. Forced into hiding, he had remained concealed ever since.

Now, the following morning, he would embark on a journey to the King's doorstep, summoned without understanding why. What could the King desire, other than to execute the last living heir to the throne? Overwhelmed by sorrow, he laid his head upon the worn and dirty table, tears streaming down his face.

Come to the Table

Morning arrived too soon for Mephibosheth, yet the end of his life seemed imminent. However, the messenger who had come for him displayed unexpected kindness when escorting him to King David's table.

Unable to contain his curiosity, Mephibosheth voiced his inquiry, "Why would you want anything to do with a worthless, insignificant creature like me?"

The response that followed forever transformed Mephibosheth's existence. Years of concealment, years of merely scraping by, all dissolved with a single word of mercy from King David. Now, he found himself seated at the King's table in a place of honor and permanence. How could this be?

* * *

Did you catch the way Mephibosheth saw himself? He referred to himself as a dead dog, a reflection of the lies that life had impressed upon him. Circumstances and the words of others had conspired to strip him of his true identity and belonging.

This story captivates me. Once, my husband preached a sermon titled "There's Room at the Table for You," which sparked within my heart the story you are reading now. Mephibosheth was a lowly man, disabled since childhood when his nurse, in a frantic attempt to escape, dropped him, leaving him crippled for life. One day, David sought to uncover any surviving descendants of Saul, and Mephibosheth was discovered and brought to the palace.

His circumstances and life experiences had caused him to live outside of his true identity, burdened by negative self-perceptions. Have you ever found yourself in a similar situation? What thoughts have your circumstances planted in your mind?

Ah, the voices ... Have you listened to them? Perhaps you have heard their echoes, saying "I can't believe I've made the same mistake again. I will never be enough. I'll never measure up. No one cares about me; I am insignificant. I can't do anything right. I'm not as attractive as others; I'll never fit in. I am a nobody, incapable of accomplishing anything. I should have seen that coming; I'm so foolish."

These voices within you, these thoughts that drown out your own voice, restrict you, hold you back, and suffocate your authenticity. I imagine Mephibosheth wrestled with similar thoughts. I know I have. Have you?

But here's where the story takes a beautiful turn. In a single day, Mephibosheth transcended from being a nobody, voiceless and forgotten, to sitting at the King's table. He moved from a place of exclusion and despair to residing within the palace. His true identity was restored as a member of the royal family. He possessed a designated place at the King's table, one he did not have to fight for or yearn after—a seat of honor that was rightfully his.

Can you fathom it? The King's table, where his sons and daughters gather, partaking in abundant meals. It is a place of honor, peace, rest, joy, and celebration. My friend, you have a place at that table where you are truly seen and heard. Your voice matters to the King of Kings and the Lord of Lords.

Can you envision it? You do not need to strive for a seat at this table, nor do you require wealth, a large following, or a particular appearance. You belong here, at this table. Release the struggles and relinquish the striving, for when you take your seat, everything finds its place. Your voice resonates, and you are seen, loved, and safe. As a beloved daughter of God, a co-heir with Jesus, his cherished bride, you are royalty. You can lay down all your burdens there. Jesus eagerly awaits your arrival, beckoning you to sit with him at his table.

* * *

Come to the Table

Tully was sitting at the kitchen table, cradling her baby girl, when the shrill ring of the phone shattered the silence. It was the call she had been expecting. Someone was on their way to pick her up and take her to her father's house—it was time. The biting cold nipped at Tully's nose as she hurriedly walked, her struggle to hold back tears palpable. Each step led her closer to the door and what awaited her on the other side—her father's life extinguished, passed from this world to the next.

As Tully sat there, tears streaming down her face, a deluge of memories flooded her mind, the echoes of the past year. Her father, at the tender age of forty-four, had been diagnosed with a merciless cancer. His time on earth was abruptly limited. Tully had fervently prayed for years, yearning for her father's salvation and a restoration of their fractured relationship. In God's mysterious ways, that devastating cancer diagnosis became the catalyst for exactly that.

She had spent many nights and days with her father, reading scripture passages, speaking of Jesus, and listening to his accounts of extraordinary visions during his darkest hours. Tully treasured those moments, knowing she would cling to those memories for the rest of her life. For the first time, she felt the warmth of a genuine connection with her father, only for him to be taken so soon.

As they came to carry her father's lifeless body away, Tully stepped outside, her steps heavy and slow. She was acutely aware that this might be her last glimpse of her father's beloved farm and the land he held so dear. On her way out, she recalled someone callously making the remark that she was now truly an orphan. Those words etched themselves into Tully's heart and would haunt her for years.

Not long after, in the middle of her pain and grief, her mother reached out, expressing a desire to see her. Tully, desperate for companionship and reassurance that she was not alone in the world, hesitantly agreed. Six years had passed since they had last spoken, and surely things had changed. Yet, Tully established clear boundaries for their meeting.

However, she soon discovered that things had not changed at all, as her mother once again vanished from her life after just a few months. The hope to which she had clung, the hope of a meaningful relationship with at least one of her parents, faded away. Tully had given it her all, gone the distance, and yearned for reconciliation. She felt lost, abandoned, and alone once more.

The word "orphan" reverberated in her ears, oppressing her voice and spirit. She questioned whether she had done enough, whether she was enough, and whether she could ever be enough. The uncertainty gnawed at her, casting doubt on her ability to be a good mother.

Despite her turmoil, Tully found solace in her roles as a wife and mother. She felt as if she needed to fade into the background, unseen and unheard. Would she ever rediscover her voice? Would she ever find a place at a table where she truly belonged, where love enveloped her without the need to fight for recognition? With time, Tully would reclaim her sense of purpose and her voice.

* * *

The woman arrived in town, keeping her distance from others. The shame and humiliation she carried were unbearable. She felt like an outcast, unseen and unheard. Years had passed, and she had silently borne her pain, burying it deep within her bones and soul. The thought that things would never be right again haunted her.

She allowed herself fleeting moments of hope—glimmers of light, promises made. Every time she heard of a new healer or doctor, she dared to trust and try once more. But after twelve long years, she had exhausted all her resources. She yearned for healing and for her troubles to cease, but she had resigned herself to fade into the background of life. Being near her was enough to make others unclean, so she believed she had no place in this world. She felt voiceless and abandoned, but she longed for a sense of belonging.

Then she saw him passing by. She couldn't explain what led her to that place, to venture where he would be that day—it was a difficult task for one in her condition. She had heard rumors of the healer, some even calling him the Messiah. Yet, she refused to let hope seep in; she simply couldn't bear another disappointment. Besides, if he asked for money, there would be no hope left, for she had nothing. She wasn't even sure how she would find her next meal.

The dreams she had once cherished—of work, love, a fulfilling life, and motherhood—had long been buried. They belonged to someone else now, not her. Lost in thoughts of her faded dreams, she suddenly heard the approaching crowd. Could it be him?

The multitude pressed around him, but she kept her distance. Then, with her own eyes, she witnessed the healing that required no payment. Blind eyes opened, and the lame walked—it sparked a glimmer of hope within her once more. Oh, if only she could be made whole! But how could she reach him? He couldn't touch her; she would have to touch him.

This was her do-or-die moment. On her hands and knees, she crawled through the throng of people. With her head down, she pressed forward. Her goal was to touch the hem of his garment. If she could just reach him, it would be enough. She had to believe; she had to press on. She had to get to him.

Every fiber of her being screamed in pain—her knees, her hands, her spirit battling against her mind, urging her to stop and surrender to despair. But deep in her heart, she knew he was the one who could set her free.

She was nearly there now. Catching a glimpse of him, she stretched out her hand as far as it would go. She simply believed. At that moment, she knew. It was finally over. Finally, she was free.

Lying there with tears of joy streaming down her face, still unseen, still unheard, but filled with an overwhelming sense of joy, she realized that even though it had taken every ounce of energy to reach him, she now felt a surge of life within her—a vitality she hadn't experienced since childhood.

Trembling in shock, she heard him call out for the one who had touched him. Surely, he couldn't be referring to her; there were so many people around. But as the crowd parted, she realized she was no longer hidden. He was talking directly to her. He could see her.

His words reverberated through her, filling her with indescribable joy. "Daughter, be comforted. Your faith has made you whole. Go in peace." It was a day of sweet peace. All her previous efforts had been in vain, and just when all hope seemed lost, there he was—with her healing, her voice, her seat at the table.

* * *

My dear sister, I know you have more than likely walked through your fair share of hardships in life. Perhaps it was a broken relationship with a friend, family member, spouse, or co-worker. Perhaps it was the loss of someone, and the grief and pain are too hard to carry. Maybe you endured trauma or battled illness. Perhaps you were hurt by someone within a church or someone close to you. It may have made you feel like you had nothing worthwhile to say, that all the hurt had finally caught up with you.

You might be in a season of life where you have lost yourself in caring for others or simply trying to survive. But no matter what has happened, who has walked away, how many times you've tried and failed, how much you blame yourself or believe you did something wrong, Jesus can meet you there. Right in the midst of it all—chaos, mess, ordinary days, extraordinary days, pain, hurt, wrongs—he is there waiting for you.

Just press on toward him, push through the crowds, and silence the noise in your head. He's already there, waiting for you to reach out and receive. He sees you, hears you, cares for you, and loves you. Rediscover your voice, find your place, and rekindle your dreams, for he makes all things new.

Let me tell you that you are unique and special. Everything you've been through can be a story that saves someone else. Your voice matters to this world and your generation. It truly matters. Whatever the enemy has thrown your way, make a promise today. Don't let it steal your voice anymore. It may take healing, support, and help, but your voice is waiting to be heard. Someone out there is waiting for you to show up to hear your voice. Their survival might just depend on it. You may think you have no voice or nothing to give, but you do, sister. Somewhere, someone is waiting for you to show up so they can survive too.

JOURNAL REFLECTION
Reclaiming Your Voice

Reflection

In this chapter, we encountered the story of a woman who had been suffering in silence for years, carrying the weight of shame, humiliation, and physical affliction. She had lost her voice, her place in society, and her hope. But in her despair, she heard about a healer, a man who had the power to bring restoration and transformation. With a glimmer of hope, she dared to believe that he could set her free.

As I reflect on this chapter, I can't help but see my own struggles mirrored in the woman's story. There have been times when I felt unseen and unheard, carrying pain and trauma deep within my being. I've experienced moments of despair, when it seemed like all hope was lost, and my dreams were buried. It's in those moments that this scripture from Psalm 34:18 becomes especially meaningful. "The Lord is close to the brokenhearted and saves those who are crushed in spirit."

This verse reminds me that even in the depths of our pain, God is near. He sees our brokenness and has the power to bring healing and restoration to our lives. The woman in the story pressed through the crowds, determined to touch the hem of Jesus' garment. She believed that just a touch could make her whole. When she reached out in faith, she experienced a miraculous transformation.

Today, I'm encouraged to press on, to press through the noise and the doubts that may be plaguing my mind. Like that woman, I need to reach out to Jesus, believing that he can bring healing and wholeness to my life. It may require vulnerability, humility, and a deep trust in God's power, but I am reminded that He is the one who can set me free.

Journal Prompts

In what ways can you relate to the struggles of the woman in this chapter? How have you felt unseen or unheard in your own life?

_____
_____
_____
_____
_____
_____
_____
_____
_____
_____
_____

Take a moment to reflect on a specific area of pain or brokenness in your life. How does the promise in Psalm 34:18 bring comfort and hope to your situation? _____

_____
_____
_____
_____
_____
_____
_____
_____

Come to the Table

What steps can you take to press on toward Jesus, even in doubt or despair? How can you reach out in faith, believing that he can bring healing and restoration to your life? _____

_____
_____
_____
_____
_____
_____
_____
_____
_____
_____

Reflect on a time when you experienced a touch from God, a moment of transformation or healing. How did that impact your faith and your perspective on your struggles? _____

_____
_____
_____
_____
_____
_____
_____
_____
_____
_____
_____

Prayer

Heavenly Father,

Thank you for being close to the brokenhearted and for saving those who are crushed in spirit. Today, I bring my pain, struggles, and brokenness before you. I confess my need for your healing touch and restoration. Help me to press on, to reach out in faith, and to trust that you can make me whole. Give me the strength and courage to embrace my voice, find my place, and pursue the dreams you have placed within me.

In Jesus' name, I pray.

Amen.

Jesus eagerly awaits your arrival, beckoning you to sit with him at his table.

CHAPTER 5

The Table of Serenity: Finding Stillness Within

Tully had spent her entire life longing for a place at the table. She wanted a table where she could be seen, heard, and esteemed above all others—a table of success.

Competition, ambition, and the pursuit of being first had driven her every move. From achieving straight A's in high school to becoming valedictorian, she constantly outperformed those around her. It was an unspoken obligation that she felt she had to fulfill.

Being number one meant recognition, validation, and a sense of belonging. She fought tirelessly day after day, believing that earning her spot would also earn her love. She had to be perfect, work relentlessly, and strive to be noticed and make others proud. Outwardly, everything appeared perfect as she masked the darkness that plagued her inner self.

Sitting at this table of success seemed gratifying. Week after week, Tully found her name at the top of the leaderboard. People applauded her achievements and marveled at her accomplishments. How could this be a negative thing? After all, isn't success what everyone should strive for? Shouldn't people work hard, give their all, and secure a prosperous life?

Despite the applause, however, Tully carried an overwhelming burden of shame, guilt, and exhaustion. How could something she had always desired lead to such imbalance? How had she ended up in this place? The table of success had left her with an unbalanced life and profound weariness. The constant guilt and shame were like enticing bait, promising a beautiful reward but ensnaring her in their grasp.

She convinced herself that she pursued success for the sake of her family's financial stability. It was her way of finding security and significance. But one day, her children faced trouble, and they needed her undivided attention. It was the first of many seasons in which Tully had to surrender and trust God with the next steps.

That day, she walked away from her office without looking back. Helping her children through their darkest times would demand all her strength and faith. Once again, she tried to fix everything on her own, just as she always had. But God showed her that only He could mend what was broken. She simply had to surrender it all to Him.

This experience marked the beginning of a season in which Tully embraced God like never before, discovering her true identity and realizing how God could use every broken piece and every moment of strife for her ultimate good.

Several years passed before Tully could fully grasp how God intended for her to respond—to rest in Him and His love. She realized that she didn't have to constantly strive to earn God's love, make Him proud, or have a voice in the world. All she had to do was embrace her identity as His daughter.

In the chaos of her life, on an ordinary night, God whispered to Tully's heart once more, and her eyes were finally opened to the truth. That night, Tully found herself watching a movie.

During her recent struggles, Tully desperately needed to relax and let go. Having recently quit her full-time job, it had been challenging for her to find peace and trust in God's plan. As she watched the movie *Ragamuffin*, she witnessed the story of Richie Mullins.

Come to the Table

Richie Mullins was a young man who struggled for years with his relationship with his heavenly Father, influenced by his strained relationship with his earthly father. As a gifted songwriter, Richie would write and perform amazing songs about the greatness of God. Behind closed doors, however, he would fall apart, drowning his sorrows in alcohol and staying in constant turmoil with those who tried to get close to him. It was a cycle of seeking validation and love, striving to earn them through his music and the approval of others.

In the movie, Richie had a profound realization while listening to a sermon by Brennan Manning. It was a moment when the truth finally broke through his heart and mind—he had missed the entire point of his life. Love from his heavenly Father wasn't something he had to earn; he didn't have to be constantly doing something to deserve that love. Brennan Manning preached about the Ragamuffin Gospel, which spoke to the truth that we are all like ragamuffins—dirty, broken, and wearing tattered clothes. That was Richie. That was Tully. That was you and me.

Tully found herself deeply connected to Richie's story that night. She saw herself in his struggles—the years of striving, the tears shed, and the constant pursuit of validation. Richie tried to write beautiful songs to get people's attention and to get God's attention. He longed to make his earthly father proud and to be seen and heard by others.

The songs he wrote and sang spoke of grace, but grace was more than just a theory. It was more than mere words in a song. Grace was God's love letter to humanity, His heartbeat for each individual. Grace said to us, "God loves you no matter what you've done or what the enemy has done to you."

Tully's father used to say those words to her, and, although it was hard for her to believe, she clung to them. Grace told her that she could come to God just as she was—a ragamuffin, dirty and worn out by the world. She could come and sit at his feet, and he would be proud of her exactly as she was in that moment. She was his chosen one, the object of his affection. He looked at her and said, "I love you, child. You don't have to do anything. You don't have to do it all. You don't have to earn my love or my grace. It is free. You just have to accept it."

The sermon Richie heard from Brennan Manning that night posed a profound question: "Did you really believe that I loved you?" It was a question from our heavenly Father, a question He asks each one of us. He knows everything about us—the good, the bad, the disappointments, and the self-doubts. Yet, despite it all, he loves us unconditionally. He was saying to Tully and says the same to all of us today, "Rest in my love. You don't have to figure it all out. You don't have to run yourself ragged. Take off those dirty, tattered, torn clothes, my child. Let me clothe you in righteousness, in robes of righteousness that are yours the moment you accept what Jesus did for you on the cross."

As Tully accepted this truth, she embraced the rest and stillness of knowing that God loved her. She didn't have to strive to do it all or be everything. She simply had to receive God's grace. It was truly amazing. Jesus had forgiven all her wrongs, and He could heal all her hurts. Tully chose to no longer hold on to her past burdens. Instead, she chose to rest in His love, rest in His grace, and experience the freedom and peace that came with it.

Tully finally had a profound realization—she had been missing the whole point all along. Jesus had been with her, rescuing her, showing her his light and love, and constantly trying to heal her. He was here with her now, demonstrating the depth of his love. Tully had accepted Jesus as her Savior, but she hadn't fully grasped the overwhelming love that said, "No matter what, you'll never be able to do enough to make me prouder or make me love you any more than I already do. I've always been proud of you. I've always loved ced21 this much. I've always wanted to fill the deepest parts of you. No matter what, I've always loved you."

Tully needed to release all her burdens and accept that Jesus loved her and was proud of her simply because she was his daughter. Due to not fully receiving the love she had needed from her earthly parents, she had believed that she had to earn God's love too. She had sung the song, "Yes, Jesus loves me," but hadn't fully believed or accepted that he could love her just as she was.

Deep in her soul, she still felt unlovable and believed that she needed to earn his love. However, in that moment, she realized that Jesus loved her and her children more than she could ever comprehend. This realization would change everything for her.

Tully had been grappling with the orphan spirit her entire life. The orphan spirit whispers that they don't belong, that they are unloved and unwanted. Even if orphans are adopted, they often still feel like outsiders within the family, like they are treated differently than the "true" children. Orphans struggle to accept and recognize love due to their experiences of abandonment. They don't hold themselves in high regard. Only by realizing her identity in Christ can someone with an orphan spirit begin to heal and allow God's truth to penetrate the depths of her heart.

Friend, even if you had both parents at home, there comes a point in life when you realize that you were an orphan too. This world is not your home. At some point, we all feel abandoned by it. The good news is that, when you know God as your Abba Father, you can embrace the knowledge that you are no longer an orphan. You don't have to live in that state any longer. You have a seat at the table.

Tully realized that everything she had done in her life had been driven by the need to earn love—love from people, her family, and her heavenly Father. In each career she pursued, she worked to make it on her own terms, exhausting herself in the process. The striving came in relentless waves, just like the Israelites wandering in circles in the wilderness, yearning to escape the barrenness and reach the promised land.

Tully had believed that she had to earn the Father's love, thinking she had to do it all on her own. After all, she had felt alone for most of her life, felt responsible for taking care of herself and earning someone's love. The memories flooded back—being called an orphan, along with cycles of pain and grief. She had operated out of insecurity, jealousy, pain, and fear. Fear had held her captive for far too long, even though Jesus had healed and rescued her. But now, it was time to let it all go. It was time to reclaim everything the enemy had stolen from her.

Once again, she surrendered it all to God in complete abandonment. She had grown tired of doing things her way, exhausted from striving. The time had come for the rhythms of rest and grace to permeate her life. She was no longer an orphan striving to earn her worth—she was a cherished daughter of God.

With sweet surrender, Tully embraced the truth that she was loved beyond measure and that her identity was firmly rooted in her heavenly Father.

* * *

She moved swiftly through the house, her mind consumed with a sense of urgency. Every corner had to be cleaned, every detail perfected. An important guest was on the way, and she wanted everything to be flawless. She had woken up earlier than usual, dedicating herself to baking and cleaning. The noon hour had arrived, and exhaustion weighed heavily on her. So much remained to be done. How would she ever manage to accomplish it all?

As the weariness settled in, she paused for a moment of reflection. She realized that, despite her fatigue and the constant busyness, she always managed to complete her tasks. Day after day, she pushed through the exhaustion and focused on the work at hand. The promise of a perfect setting for the guest's arrival kept her going. She anticipated praise for her efforts and hoped to earn favor, recognition, and love.

Even after the guests arrived, she continued to race around, maintaining her frantic pace. And then, it hit her. Her sister, Mary, had been lending a hand here and there, but she seemed carefree and found joy in singing and simply being present. Mary embraced a whimsical nature, seemingly unburdened by the weight of responsibilities. Martha couldn't bear it any longer. Frustration and resentment welled up within her and burst forth in words she would soon regret.

But Jesus quickly intervened, reminding Martha of her preoccupation with many things. In contrast, Mary had chosen the one thing that truly mattered—leaning in, gathering up the goodness of God. Blinded by her busyness and worry, Martha had almost missed it.

* * *

Sister, does this resonate with you in your current season of life? Are you perpetually consumed by worries and concerns? Do you constantly strive to find solutions to life's never-ending problems? Is your busyness an attempt to drown out the pain that lurks in the silence?

When was the last time you simply sat still, releasing control and surrendering it all to Jesus? Perhaps, for some of you, that moment has never come. From a young age, you felt the need to earn your worth in the face of abandonment, fighting against the world. Every moment of your life seemed to require relentless striving—for yourself, for your children, or for others.

You might even find yourself like the widow woman seeking healing, with hope dwindling and nothing left. You can't see a way out, and the absence of answers drives you to worry and work even harder. Prayer takes a backseat as time for self-care or studying God's word becomes scarce.

I understand. Truly, I do. But can I share something with you? You don't have to figure it all out alone. In fact, trying to do so will only prolong the process. God surrounds you at this very moment. He places people in your life to offer assistance. The more you surrender to him, the more time you spend in his presence, the more you'll discover his miracles working all around you. Somehow, everything will fall into place, though perhaps not in the way you expect. God's ways are not our ways; his thoughts are higher.

Trade your worries for his peace today. Exchange your striving for rest in him. Swap your sorrow for his joy. It's as simple as saying, "Jesus, you can have it all." In that very moment, you'll encounter the quiet, still voice that will guide you along the way—his way, the perfect way.

One of the most effective ways to combat worry and trust God is to focus on his promises in the Bible. When worry takes hold, take a few moments to read and meditate on his word. Remind yourself of the countless times God has faithfully shown up in the past. By fixating on his faithfulness and promises, you'll cultivate trust in him instead of succumbing to worry.

Journaling your worries through prayer is another powerful tool for releasing them to him. When the weight becomes too heavy, turn up the praise music, go for a long walk, and let it all out. Engage in daily gratitude, thanking him in advance for the blessings yet to come. Through this practice, your faith will grow, and your focus will shift toward hope for the future.

Learning to rest in God and his grace demands intentional effort to quiet your mind and connect with Him. It requires cutting out distractions and granting yourself grace throughout the process. Prioritize God each day, and you'll discover a strength that can only come from him. Evaluate everything in your life—determine what is truly necessary, and release the unnecessary burdens that hinder your ability to rest in who you are and your calling in him.

Make time for daily mindfulness and prayer. Mindful moments with God involve becoming aware of your thoughts, feelings, and physical sensations while being completely open and honest with him. Through daily prayer, you can express your needs and rely on his help. Seek solace in nature and the great outdoors. Take breaks throughout the day to rest and relax.

Remember, being still in God's presence requires effort on your part. Resting in him is not a passive act but a powerful and meaningful experience. It involves taking time to be still, allowing yourself to experience his peace, and listening to his voice. It may entail prayer, reading the Bible, journaling, or simply sitting in stillness with him. Resting in God deepens your connection with him and renews your spirit.

Embrace the truth. Be still and know that he is God. Pause, reflect, and be mindful of God's power and presence in your life. Trust in him, regardless of the challenges you face. Rest in the assurance that God is always with you and in control. Surrender to him. Trust in his promise that, when you seek him first, everything else will fall into place. It is the greatest secret to daily success and abundant living—a secret waiting for you to put into practice.

JOURNAL REFLECTION
Trading Worry for Rest in God

"Come unto me, all ye that labour and are heavy laden, and I will give you rest." (Matthew 11:28, KJV)

Reflection

In our journey through this chapter, we have encountered a profound theme—the invitation to trade our worries for rest in God. This theme resonates deeply within us, as we often find ourselves burdened by the weight of anxiety and the never-ending quest for control. Today, let's delve deeper into this theme and discover the transformative power of finding rest in our heavenly Father.

The words of Jesus in Matthew 11:28 ring with timeless relevance: "Come to me, all you who are weary and burdened, and I will give you rest." These words carry a divine promise—a promise of respite from the weariness and heaviness that life often brings. Jesus invites us into His embrace, offering solace, comfort, and peace that surpasses all understanding.

Worry has a way of entangling our thoughts and ensnaring our hearts, leaving us restless and anxious. But, as we respond to the call of Jesus, we choose to lay our burdens at his feet and exchange our worries for the rest that only he can provide. This act of surrender requires trust—deep, unwavering trust in God's character and his steadfast love for us.

Journal Prompts

Trading worry for rest begins with anchoring ourselves in God's promises. We find them within the pages of his Word, where he reassures us of his faithfulness, provision, and care. Take time each day to immerse yourself in Scripture, allowing God's promises to take root in your heart. Write them down, reflect on them, and let them become a source of strength and comfort in times of uncertainty.

What are the worries or burdens that you find yourself carrying today? Take a moment to name them and write them down. _____
_____
_____
_____
_____
_____
_____
_____
_____
_____

In what ways have these worries impacted your life? How have they hindered your sense of peace and rest? _____
_____
_____
_____
_____
_____
_____
_____
_____
_____

Come to the Table

What specific promises from God's Word bring you comfort and hope? Write down one or two verses that resonate with you. _____
_____
_____
_____
_____
_____
_____
_____
_____

How can you incorporate regular time in God's Word into your daily routine? What practical steps can you take to ensure that you anchor yourself in his promises?

In prayer, we find a sacred space to release our worries and find solace in God's presence. Approach him with a humble and open heart, pouring out your concerns, fears, and anxieties before him. As you surrender them, trust that he is listening, he understands, and he is working all things together for your good. In the stillness of prayer, allow his peace to wash over you, soothing your restless soul. _____
_____
_____
_____
_____
_____
_____
_____

How often do you bring your worries and concerns before God in prayer? Are there any barriers or distractions that hinder you from fully surrendering them to him? _____

_____
_____
_____
_____
_____
_____
_____
_____

Take a moment to lay your worries before God in prayer right now. Give him permission to carry them for you and ask for his peace to fill your heart. Finding rest in God also involves cultivating a lifestyle of mindfulness and stillness. During our fast-paced lives, it is essential to create intentional moments of quiet reflection. Carve out time each day to simply be in God's presence—undistracted and fully present. Open your heart and ears to listen to his gentle whispers, guiding you and speaking words of comfort and assurance. In these moments, let go of the need to control. Instead, allow God to take the reins, knowing that his plans are perfect and his ways are higher than ours. _____

_____
_____
_____
_____
_____
_____
_____
_____

How can you create intentional moments of stillness and reflection in your daily life? What practical steps can you take to cultivate a lifestyle of mindfulness in God's presence? _____

_____
_____
_____
_____
_____
_____
_____
_____
_____
_____

What do you sense God speaking to you in this quiet moment? Is there a specific area of your life where he is inviting you to surrender control and find rest in him? _____

_____
_____
_____
_____
_____
_____
_____
_____
_____
_____
_____

As you respond to the theme of trading worries for rest in God, remember that it is not a one-time event but a continuous journey. It requires intentional choices and a daily commitment to trust in him. When worry threatens to consume you, remind yourself of the promise Jesus made—he will give you rest. Seek him earnestly, and he will embrace you with his peace.

May this be a gentle reminder that you are not alone in your worries. Your heavenly Father is ready to exchange your burdens for his rest. Trust in his love, hold fast to his promises, and find solace in his presence. May you experience the transformative power of trading worry for rest, and may your soul be refreshed by the peace that surpasses all understanding.

Prayer

Gracious Father,

I come before you, weary and burdened, longing for your rest. Thank you for the invitation to trade my worries for your peace. Help me to anchor my heart in your promises, to pour out my concerns before you in prayer, and to cultivate stillness and mindfulness in your presence. Guide me on this journey of trading worry for rest, and fill my soul with your peace that surpasses all understanding.

In Jesus' name, I pray.

Amen.

The words of Jesus in Matthew 11:28 ring with timeless relevance: "Come to me, all you who are weary and burdened, and I will give you rest."

CHAPTER 6

The Table of Clarity: Deciphering Your Purpose

If you haven't already figured it out, I am Tully. It's my story that I've told you throughout this book. I shared my story in this way because I want you to realize that you have a story to tell too. Even if you have to put a name to it that isn't yours to help you process and heal through it, even if it's hard to write out or tell others, know that you can. Know that you have a voice and that God truly can take the pain and help you heal, help others heal, help you find purpose in it. You can take every bit of what the enemy throws at you and make it into a fiery dart to fire right back at him by using your voice to make a difference for someone else.

My greatest purpose in life is to point others to a closer walk with Jesus, to know him and make him known, to allow God to use all that the enemy tried to destroy me with for the purpose of helping someone—someone just like you—to know that, no matter what, you matter, you are loved, you are redeemed, and you belong.

In reflecting upon my journey, I have realized that I was rescued to rescue. This revelation holds for you as well. You are not defined by your past or the pain you have endured. You are a cherished daughter of God, his glorious creation, the object of his affection, and the recipient of his grace. He loves you unconditionally, and you are the apple of his eye.

Come to the Table

Take a moment now to let God remind you of who you truly are. Release all the burdens and imperfections of your past and place them at his feet. It may be messy, loud, or imperfect, but that's okay. Take your time. Be gentle with yourself day by day.

What is not okay is allowing your past to hinder you from embracing your true identity and fulfilling your purpose. The enemy wants to use your life's challenges to distract you, to make you believe that you are not good enough, and to convince you that you can never make a difference. These are all lies.

Today, you stand at the table of decision—a pivotal moment in your life. Just as you have made decisions at various tables throughout your life, this particular table is different. It is the table where you decide to heal, step into your true identity, and recognize the impact your life has on others. It is a table where you discover the purpose woven throughout your story and how you can create significant moments with Jesus, just as Peter experienced his water-walking moment.

* * *

In his turmoil and uncertainty, Peter found himself unable to sleep. His mind was filled with questions about his identity, the men in the boat with him, and the purpose behind it all. The storm within him mirrored the storm raging around him.

In the darkness, he caught sight of a glimmer of light—a figure walking on water. Was it a ghost? At that moment, Peter realized that Jesus was the answer for which he had been searching.

He called out to Jesus and made a decision. He chose to step out of the boat and walk on water toward him. Though he momentarily lost focus and began to sink, Jesus reached out his hand and pulled him up. Peter learned the importance of keeping his eyes fixed on Jesus.

Friend, Jesus will never let go of you. Even when life's waves threaten to knock you down and the storms of life rage around you, as long as you hold on to Jesus, he will hold on to you. Others may walk away, and the enemy may try to convince you that you are alone, but the truth remains—Jesus will always be there for you, fighting on your behalf and standing by your side. Keep your eyes fixed on him and find solace in his presence.

It is time to leave the past behind and step into your true identity and purpose. Release the old labels and embrace who you are—a child of the King who is redeemed, chosen, and called by name.

As I journeyed through my healing, I came to understand that not everything happens for a reason. It is difficult to accept the notion that God had a reason for the pain and suffering inflicted upon us. The truth is, bad things happen because we live in a fallen world, and the enemy seeks to destroy what God holds dear.

God's original plan was for us to experience a pain-free existence, enjoy His creation, and have a close relationship with Him. However, the enemy disrupted this plan, and God responded by sending Jesus to bring restoration and redemption to his children.

The work Jesus accomplished on the cross, the grace he extended to us through that act, enables us to be restored to a perfect relationship with God. One day, Jesus will return, and we will enter into a new heaven and a new earth, where there will be no more sorrow, pain, or bad things. The thought of that glorious day should fill our hearts with hope and anticipation. Let us prepare ourselves, declaring that we are no longer slaves but children of God, ready to embrace the unimaginable and indescribable things he has prepared for us.

Remember, you are not alone on this path. God is with you, guiding and transforming you day by day. Trust in his love and allow him to make all things new in your life.

As we journey through the process of healing and transformation, it is crucial to confront those profound questions that shape our lives. Again, stop and ask yourself, "Who am I, and what am I called to do?" What does God's word say about who you are and what you are called to do? These questions hold the key to understanding your true identity, purpose, and potential for growth and impact.

It is natural to wonder whether God can make something good out of the pain, hurt, and mistakes we have experienced. The answer is a resounding "Yes!" We can hold on to the truth of Romans 8:28, which assures us that God works all things together for the good of those who love him and are called according to his purpose.

I am a living testament to this truth. Despite the challenges and mistakes in my own life, God has brought about unexpected blessings and healing. I recognize that my journey could have taken a different path, but by God's grace, I chose to come into agreement with him, to embrace his love and grace.

When faced with pain and trauma, many individuals allow the enemy to take their pain and amplify its destructive effects. But you have a choice. What have you done with your pain? Have you made peace with it, or have you allowed it to hinder you from embracing your true identity and calling? Have you buried it so deep that it has numbed your emotions and prevented you from living fully?

Choosing to stay at tables where we don't belong, where we are labeled by whispered lies, leads us into religion rather than a true relationship with God. It's time to turn the tables and flip them upside down. Release the need to fight for a seat at the wrong table, and embrace the healing journey God has for you.

Sometimes, pain and trauma leave deep wounds that need to be acknowledged and healed. The word "trauma" itself comes from the Greek word meaning "wound." Just like physical wounds, unhealed pain and trauma can numb us, disconnect us from ourselves and others, and distort our view of our own identity. Stress and trauma can also take a toll on our well-being when they manifest in physical and mental health conditions.

But take heart, for the enemy's plan to exhaust and distract you from God's purpose can be overcome. God's light shines brightest in the darkness, and it is his love and grace that bring healing and restoration. Don't let the wounds of the past extinguish the light within you. Surrender all that you've been through to God. Lay everything at his feet, and allow him to begin the necessary work of healing and restoration in your life.

In today's world, it's easy to be distracted and disconnected from our true selves and our Creator. We try to fill the emptiness within us with various external pursuits, but true healing and purpose can only be found in God. It is up to us to show up, to bring our pain to the light, and to allow God's love to overcome all the hurt, pain, and wrong in our lives.

Make the decision today to approach God's table of healing and restoration. Surrender everything to him. Renounce the lies, the spirits of oppression, and the false identities the enemy has tried to impose upon you. Reclaim your true identity as a daughter of the King—chosen, redeemed, and set free. Rise above the captivity of the enemy and embrace your purpose and calling.

Remember, you are not alone in this journey. God has connected you with others who will support you, and you will have the opportunity to support and serve them as well. Rise as the warrior woman you are, drawing the line against the enemy's captivity. Commit to living out your purpose and serving others with love and devotion.

One of the greatest challenges we face is making peace with our past. The wounds, mistakes, and pain of yesterday often linger in our minds and hearts, clouding our perception of the present and hindering us from stepping into our purpose. But it doesn't have to be this way. We have the power to make peace with our past and find purpose in the present.

Take a moment to reflect on your past experiences, both the positive and the negative. What are the moments that have shaped you? What are the lessons you've learned? Allow yourself to acknowledge the pain and hurt but also recognize the strength and resilience that have brought you to where you are today.

The Word tells us, "Remember ye not the former things, neither consider the things of old. Behold, I will do a new thing; now it shall spring forth; shall ye not know it? I will even make a way in the wilderness, and rivers in the desert." (Isaiah 43:18-19, KJV)

Forgiveness is a powerful tool for making peace with the past. It is not only about forgiving others but also about forgiving ourselves. Release any resentment, guilt, or shame that may be holding you back. Understand that forgiveness does not mean condoning the actions or forgetting the past but, rather, choosing to let go and move forward.

We are reminded that, "even as Christ forgave us, so also we should forgive." (Colossians 3:13, KJV)

Forgiving someone doesn't mean that you condone their actions or behavior, it doesn't mean that you have to allow them into your personal space or into your life, there are still consequences to every action. I can forgive someone and still maintain healthy boundaries. As you learn to forgive others for the past, and forgive yourself too your heart will begin to heal.

Realize that your past does not define you. Each day is an opportunity to live out your purpose, regardless of what you've been through. Seek God's guidance and ask him to reveal his plans for your life. Embrace the present moment, and be open to the possibilities and opportunities that lie before you. "For we are God's handiwork, created in Christ Jesus to do good works, which God prepared in advance for us to do." (Ephesians 2:10)

Remember that God can bring beauty out of ashes and turn our pain into purpose. Trust in his sovereignty, and believe that he is working all things together for your good. Even in uncertainty, trust that he has a plan and purpose for your life that far exceed your past experiences.

As you embark on the journey of making peace with your past and finding purpose in the present, know that you are not alone. Lean on God, seek his wisdom, and surround yourself with a supportive community that can encourage and uplift you along the way.

As we conclude this chapter, let us embark on the journey of self-discovery, embracing our true identity and purpose. Let the healing begin. May the embrace of God's love propel us forward into a life filled with joy, fulfillment, and transformative impact. You are a beloved daughter of the King—embrace your true identity and step into the incredible purpose he has for you.

JOURNAL REFLECTION
Embracing Your Identity and Purpose

Reflection

Take your time to reflect on these questions and allow the Holy Spirit to guide your thoughts and responses. Remember, journaling is a personal journey of self-discovery and growth. Be honest with yourself and open to the transformative work God wants to do in your life. May this reflection bring you closer to understanding and embracing your true identity and purpose in him.

Journal Prompts

What resonated with you the most in this chapter? Why do you think it had such an impact on you? _____

_____
_____
_____
_____
_____
_____
_____
_____
_____
_____

Reflect on a time when you allowed pain, hurt, or past mistakes to hinder you from fully embracing your identity and purpose. How did it make you feel? What do you think God's perspective on that situation would be? _____

_____
_____
_____
_____
_____
_____
_____

"But he said unto me, 'My grace is sufficient for thee: for my strength is made perfect in weakness.'" (2 Corinthians 12:9a, KJV)

How have you been holding on to tables in your life that don't align with your true identity? Identify any areas where you have been seeking validation from the wrong sources or allowing labels to define you. _____

_____
_____
_____
_____
_____
_____
_____

"And be not conformed to this world: but be ye transformed by the renewing of your mind, that ye may prove what is that good, and acceptable, and perfect, will of God." (Romans 12:2, KJV)

Consider any unhealed pain or trauma that has affected your life. How has it shaped your view of yourself and your relationships? In what ways has it hindered you from fully experiencing the abundant life God has for you? _____

_____
_____
_____
_____
_____
_____
_____
_____
_____

"He healeth the broken in heart, and bindeth up their wounds."
(Psalm 147:3, KJV)

What steps can you take to bring your pain and trauma to God's table of healing and restoration? How can you surrender it to him and allow him to begin the work of healing in your life? _____

_____
_____
_____
_____
_____
_____
_____
_____
_____

"Come unto me, all ye that labour and are heavy laden, and I will give you rest."
(Matthew 11:28, KJV)

Reflect on your true identity as a daughter of the King. How does it make you feel to know that you are chosen, redeemed, and set free? How does embracing this identity impact the way you approach life and fulfill your purpose? _____
_____
_____
_____
_____
_____
_____
_____
_____
_____
_____

"Behold, what manner of love the Father hath bestowed upon us, that we should be called the sons of God: therefore, the world knoweth us not, because it knew him not." (1 John 3:1a, KJV)

Prayer

Heavenly Father,

Thank you for the opportunity to reflect on your Word and the truths shared in this chapter. As I delve into my thoughts and emotions, I invite your presence to guide me and bring clarity to my reflections.

Lord, I acknowledge that there have been times when I allowed pain, hurt, and past mistakes to overshadow my identity and purpose in you. I confess that I sought validation from the wrong sources and clung to tables that do not align with your plan for my life. Forgive me for allowing these things to define me and hinder my growth.

I bring before you any unhealed pain or trauma that has influenced my perspective and impacted my relationships. I lay it all at your feet, trusting in your power to heal and restore. Help me to surrender these wounds to your table of healing and allow you to work in me.

Father, I embrace the truth that I am your beloved child. Thank you for choosing me, redeeming me, and setting me free. I am grateful for the identity you have given me in Christ. As I walk in this truth, empower me to live out my purpose and fulfill your calling on my life.

I surrender all my burdens, weariness, and brokenness to you, knowing that you are my source of rest and strength. Guide me as I seek to align my thoughts and actions with your will, and renew my mind to be transformed by your truth.

I commit to walking in the light of your love, allowing it to overcome the darkness in my life. Grant me the courage and discernment to let go of the lies of the enemy and embrace the truth of who I am in you.

Thank you for being my faithful and loving Father. I trust that you will continue to lead me on this journey of discovering and embracing my true identity and purpose. May your Holy Spirit be my constant companion, guiding me each step of the way.

In Jesus' name, I pray. Amen.

Reclaim your true identity as a daughter of the King—chosen, redeemed, and set free. Rise above the captivity of the enemy and embrace your purpose and calling.

CHAPTER 7

The Table of Redemption:
Healing the Past and Embracing the Present

All her life, she had carried the burden of feeling out of place. The weight of not belonging to the in-crowd, of being different from the others, haunted her every step. As an orphan, she was labeled a poor, pitiful girl, condemned to the whispers and pity of her people. The absence of her parents cast a shadow over her, leaving her wondering if she would ever find love or a place to call home. Was she destined to be defined by her tragedies? Yet, despite all of that, she chose to seek the good and love her people.

Among the locals, she was seen as a captive, a nobody. Their stares and talk made her uncomfortable as if she were constantly under scrutiny. The words and whispers pierced her soul, driving her to seek solace in seclusion. She felt like a prisoner trapped within her own life, longing to escape the unwanted attention.

However, in the safety of her home, she found refuge in her uncle's stories of their people and homeland. He reminded her that she was uniquely beautiful, and her name symbolized the fragrance of the life she would become. His love and words gave her strength to face each day with courage.

Her uncle's presence was her sanctuary. He was the only person she trusted in the world. The thought of losing him filled her with fear. She questioned if God had a plan for her beyond a life of hiding, slavery in a foreign land, and eternal loneliness.

As the sun rose on an ordinary day, her uncle entered with life-altering news. The queen had been banished for her actions at the king's banquet, and now the king sought a new queen. Hadassah would go to the palace, but her true identity must be hidden behind a new name.

Hadassah embraced her new identity as Esther, a name that filled her with confidence and courage. Everything seemed to unfold rapidly, and she experienced a whirlwind of emotions—fear, excitement, hopelessness, and hopefulness. Deep down, she held on to her uncle's words, believing that, perhaps, she was created for such a time as this. Could it be that she, the orphan, the captive, the stranger, held the power to save her people? The beauty that once attracted unwanted attention now captured the favor of the king.

Life within the palace was unlike anything she had ever known, yet in the grandeur, she questioned God's purpose for her. She stood at a crossroads, aware that her decision could cost her everything. To save others, she had to reveal her true identity, risking her life in the process. But within her, she knew that all the pain of her past had led her to this moment—it was her purpose. She surrendered herself to God, allowing him to transform her pain into a vessel of redemption for others.

*   *   *

The historical account of Esther in God's Word reveals how she unveiled her true identity and became a savior to her people. She emerged as one of the great heroes of the Jewish nation, a powerful testament to the transformation that can occur in the life of an orphan. From queen to heroine, her past filled with tragedy, trauma, pain, and uncertainty became a force of salvation.

Dear friend, you too can find yourself within Esther's story. In the hands of God, your journey can become a mighty instrument to save a generation. What does it take to reach such a place? It requires surrender, letting go of everything that holds you back. It necessitates examining the roots that anchor you and determining if they are hindering your growth.

Consider what you have been planted and rooted in that may be limiting you in the present. What beliefs, fears, or past experiences are holding you captive? It's time to unearth those roots, face the pain, and make peace with it. Allow God to transform your pain into purpose, for in his hands, your story can become a powerful tool to bring salvation and hope to those around you.

Remember, just as Esther surrendered to God's plan, you too can surrender it all and discover the true power of your identity rooted in him.

* * *

During a recent storm, a tornado tore through our neighborhood, wreaking havoc on our homes. Fortunately, our house sustained minimal damage, and we remained safe. However, our yard was left in shambles, resembling a warzone. Decades-old trees, once towering and majestic, were uprooted and strewn across the landscape.

As I stood next to one of these fallen giants, I couldn't help but contemplate the significance of roots—how they can be both beneficial and detrimental. Reflecting on a painful experience a few months prior, when I underwent a root canal on two teeth simultaneously (and let me tell you, I'm not the bravest when it comes to the dentist), I realized the impact of a bad root. Such a root can cause immense trouble and pain, as I had personally experienced. My fear of the dentist had prevented me from seeking timely treatment, prolonging my suffering unnecessarily. If only I had confronted the issue at the first sign of pain, I could have saved myself a great deal of trouble.

Come to the Table

Isn't it true that we often avoid facing our pain, preferring to ignore its existence and hope it vanishes on its own? Instead of seeking the guidance of experts, we try various remedies to alleviate our suffering. Removing these massive uprooted trees and their sprawling root systems from our yard was a daunting task. It was evident that we would require the assistance of professionals.

Being vertically challenged at just five feet tall on a good day, I couldn't possibly handle it myself (especially considering the towering root systems). Can you imagine me trying to do this on my strength? Yet, isn't that how silly we must look to God as we try to handle all of life on our terms, our ways, relying on our own strength?

In these thoughts, I couldn't escape the parallels between the tangled roots lying in the mud and the strongholds that labels, lies, words, trauma, false identities, and pain have on our lives. Just as the roots of a fallen tree, once a source of energy and life, can become a hindrance, our own root systems can either bind us to detrimental sources or anchor us in God's goodness. Just as a tree's roots can drain it of vitality after it has fallen, our lives can suffer when we're rooted in the wrong things. But when our roots are deeply embedded in God, they become a source of strength, nourishment, and life.

When we aren't anchored in God's truth and his healing hand, the storms of life come, and we become like that tree planted in unfavorable soil with exposed roots—a rather unsightly mess. Despite appearing beautiful on the surface just days before the storm, we tend to neglect our internal struggles, focusing solely on maintaining an attractive facade.

When we avoid dealing with pain and trauma, the result is an ugly, messy existence—a state of being knocked down by life's storms. It is only when we recognize the need for an expert that we can begin the process of healing. Thankfully, those of us who have embraced Jesus as our Savior have an ultimate expert at our disposal. Surrendering our pain to him doesn't mean the journey will be effortless or painless. It requires our active participation and can be arduous, causing soreness in our hearts and souls, much like the work of a tree expert meticulously removing roots. Sounds like heart surgery to me, how about you?

As I contemplated the trees in my yard, I realized that I faced a choice—whether to summon the expert to handle the situation or leave the fallen trees as they were. Ignoring them would lead to potential harm for others and myself. Consequently, I decided to call in the expert and entrust the task to their capable hands, despite the cost. The outcome would undoubtedly be worth it.

As I stood there, gazing at the fallen trees in my yard and pondering the potential for new life to flourish once the roots are removed, the profound implications of God's love, mercy, and grace struck me. The process of extracting those exposed roots resonated with the concept of allowing God to be our root excavator—a transformative act that comes at no cost to us, yet cost Him His beloved Son, Jesus. Reflecting on this, I realized that while the fallen trees and their upturned roots could be prepared for a new beginning, God's work of renewal in our lives is even more powerful. Just as I can envision a future of beauty in my yard, God envisions a future of abundant life for each of us. He sent His Son to liberate the captive, mend the brokenhearted, restore sight to the blind, and grant us life—a life overflowing with purpose and fulfillment.

The best news? The price for our redemption has already been paid. We've already obtained a sweet victory in Jesus.

In 2 Corinthians 1:4, the apostle Paul reminds us that God is the God of comfort, always ready to come alongside us in our pain and trials. He pours out his comfort on us so that we, in turn, can comfort others who are hurting. Our purpose in our pain is to be empowered by the Holy Spirit to empower those around us. It is a beautiful cycle of healing and restoration.

Digging up those roots, which is necessary for our growth and freedom, can feel like death to our fleshly desires. Sometimes, we become so accustomed to the pain that it becomes like a pacifier, keeping us comfortable in our brokenness. But those roots, those lies that have held us captive, need to be cut off and allowed to die. While we will never forget the pain, we will live better without it.

As we remove the old roots and prepare the soil of our hearts, we can grow new roots nourished by God's love and life-giving nutrients. Those old roots will no longer hold us back. Instead, new roots will emerge and propel us forward, enabling us to bloom with new life and stand taller and stronger than ever before. We will become like trees planted in the right spot, reflecting God's glory through the life we live.

Having a healthy root system that draws from the right nutrients and minerals changes our lives. It severs the lies of the enemy and breaks down the strongholds that keep us grounded in the wrong things. Our fleshly roots will no longer steal from us or keep us silent. Instead, we will be able to share our stories, believe in our worthiness, and embrace our identity as overcomers.

In this process of replanting, we will discover a newfound strength—a strength that replaces the beliefs that we are not enough or that we'll never measure up. We will start to trust again and find hope. Our vision and dreams will begin to take shape. We will truly believe that we are loved, not for what we do or don't do, but simply for who we are—children of God.

As we peer into the distance, we will see a beautiful table that stretches beyond our sight. There is a seat at that table with our name on it, saved specifically for us. We won't have to fight for it or question our belonging. We can rest in the glorious love of God.

Just as God promised in Isaiah 35, he will bring blooms in the desert of our lives. When we feel surrounded by barrenness and hopelessness, he invites us to look to him. He promises to provide streams in the desert, to make root systems grow, and to bring life to dry bones. Our lives will become a sweet aroma in crushing circumstances, just like Esther, who emerged from her former identity as Hadassah to become a beacon of hope and truth.

In Corinthians, Paul describes how our lives become living letters, permanently engraved by the Spirit of the living God on the tablets of our tender hearts. Through the empowering presence of God, we become sources of truth, life, and love. Our root systems bring flourishing leaves, providing comfort and shelter to those around us.

No longer will we be bound by the flesh, the enemy's words, or the traumatic experiences that have kept us hidden. We will be set free. Just as a root canal relieves the pain, our newfound freedom will remove the masks and restore our joy. Filled with the right nutrients from the Holy Spirit, we will overflow into every area of our lives—our relationships, families, communities, churches, and careers.

We will recognize that this is the moment for which we were created. We will no longer waste time wallowing in pain because there is a generation depending on us. When we make peace with our pain, we realize that there is too much at stake. We understand that there is a power within us that is greater than anything the enemy can use to destroy us—the power of God living in us.

As children of God, we always have access to that power, but sometimes we forget. We need to allow God to perform surgery, reconstruct our hearts, and excavate our roots. Only then can new life begin. We will develop new thought patterns, no longer speaking or thinking negatively about ourselves. Instead, we will become aware of our thoughts and transform them before they manifest as words.

With renewed minds, we will envision a future filled with purpose. Our thoughts will align with God's truth, and we will recognize that we are loved simply for who we are—his daughters. Our gaze will be fixed on the table he has prepared for us, knowing that we belong there.

Preparing the soil for this kind of life requires a willingness to use our stories for God's glory. It demands a deep-rooted faith that can withstand any storm. But the rewards far outweigh the effort. We will flourish, and future generations will benefit from our faithfulness.

So, my friend, I ask you: What will it take for you to prepare the soil of your heart? What will it take for you to use your story for God's glory? What will it take for you to develop a root system so deep that no storm can knock you down? Embrace the process of replanting, and watch as God brings forth new life, transforming you into a magnificent reflection of his glory.

What did it take for the great men and women of the Bible? If we look back, we can see that in every instance—Mary Magdalene, Martha, the woman at the well, Peter, Mephibosheth, the woman with the issue of blood, and Esther—it took surrender. They had to surrender their preconceived notions of how life should look and be, letting go of the world's ways and root systems. It required faith and reaching out to someone else, believing and allowing the expert to be the expert. They had to trust God with the impossible. If you thought life was glorious before, just wait until you have the right root system!

Continuing with Paul in Corinthians, he speaks of the ministry that imparts righteousness and excels in glory. The increasing glory will replace the former glory. Yes, the tree was beautiful before it fell, but the tree that will be replanted, along with the trees still standing, will be far more glorious than the fallen tree. All things will be made new again and again. Today, I wonder, will you let him make all things new for you?

You see, there is an amazing hope living within you that allows you to step into your purpose in freedom and truth. What is the truth? The pain may say it is impossible, no one really loves you, you're tired and always mess things up, you have to constantly please others to be liked, you're not capable, and you can't bear it anymore. You may feel unworthy, afraid, flawed, unable to forgive yourself, alone, and always worried or frustrated. Truth declares that all things are possible. You are deeply loved. He will give you rest and guidance. His strength is perfected in your weakness. You have been given power and a sound mind instead of fear. You are forgiven, never alone, redeemed, treasured, a daughter of God, chosen, and set apart with a purpose for such a time as this—the very moment for which you were born.

On which path will you continue? Today, God is saying to you, "Daughter, the table is just in sight. Surrender it all to me, and I will save you, help you, redeem you, and uphold you with my righteous right hand" (Isaiah 41:10). You don't have to save yourself, clean up on your own, or pretend to be something you're not. You don't have to hide. Simply trust and believe in the truth to be set free.

I want to encourage you right now to stand up and confront the pain of the past. If you can't speak it, write it out. Maybe it's a person, and perhaps you need to give that pain a name. Call it out right now, expressing gratitude for the lessons it taught you—the things you learned not to be and the things it taught you to be.

Yes, life may have dealt you some unfair hands, but today you get to choose how you will respond to it. Tell the pain that you no longer need it. Choose to walk away in peace and command it to sit down. It no longer has a hold on you. Walk away knowing that you have been given a spirit of power and a sound mind, not fear. Walk away knowing that you are walking toward your destiny and the purpose that God has for you in this very moment. Now you know that the enemy is coming to steal and destroy, but you are prepared for the battles ahead.

In 2 Corinthians 4, Paul describes how we are troubled on every side, yet not distressed; perplexed, but not in despair; persecuted, but not forsaken; cast down, but not destroyed. We carry in our bodies the dying of the Lord Jesus so that his life may be manifested in us.

Take a moment, sister, to linger there. Let the life of Jesus be made manifest in your body. Make peace with the pain and find purpose in the present. Your purpose right now is to go and do the thing God has called you to do, showing up boldly to fulfill it.

Seek help if you need it. Show the love of God to everyone around you, allowing the life of Jesus within you to shine. Let him be the sign on your forehead that says, "Love lives here. He loves me deeply, and He loves you too." The enemy may have tried to destroy us, and he will continue to do so until the end, but God has a plan, and he is our purpose.

Here are four important things to remember:

1. God has a plan for you, and the enemy will use everything in your past and present to try to keep you from following that plan.
2. God did not make a mistake in placing you where you are today.
3. Most of the time, God's plan for you won't be comfortable. It involves exposing roots, dealing with pain, choosing to forgive, choosing to love, choosing to walk in his calling, and allowing him to take all the pain and give you peace. It won't always look like what you expect, and it may make no sense to those around you.

4. The time for you to make peace with the pain, begin healing, find purpose in the present, and follow God's plan for your life is NOW.

It will take some time sitting quietly alone with God for him to reveal what that plan is. Jesus fasted for 40 days in the wilderness before his assignment, and Esther fasted for three days before approaching her assignment, so you can benefit from fasting too. Ask God, "What is it that you want to do with my life? How can you use my pain and my story to help others and lead them to you?" Whatever he says to do in that moment, go do it! "For who knows whether you have come for such a time as this?"

I can envision it now, can you? I've had the vision for years now in my mind. Picture it with me: A little girl, long brown hair wildly blowing in the wind. She is barefoot and weary, her clothes torn and tattered. Her feet ache from running for so long, and her body bears scratches, bruises, and dirt. But in the darkness, she glimpses a flicker of light.

In the distance, a table emerges. It stretches on endlessly with countless chairs. Vibrant flowers cascade over its edges, and silver and gold dishes overflow with abundance beyond her wildest dreams.

There it is now—her chair. A chair she no longer has to fight for, strive for, or earn. It's the perfect chair, reserved just for her. It bears her name. It's her rightful place, a place at the table already paid for by her redeemer, Jesus.

She now understands. She no longer needs to struggle or fight for anything she needs. She knows she has a place where she truly belongs. In that place, she feels safe, seen, and heard. She is enveloped in love. She realizes who she has always been deep down. The daughter of the King. With that understanding, she confidently takes her rightful place at the table.

Come to the Table

Sister, come to the table. You will find everything you need. Come to the table. He eagerly awaits your arrival. Come to the table, your rightful place of belonging. Leave behind the labels and lies that have plagued you. Come to the table where peace awaits. Come to the table where you can find rest. Come to the table where you are forever his.

Come to the table. Discover the abundant life that awaits you.

JOURNAL REFLECTION
Healing the Past and Embracing the Present

Reflection

Reflect on the following verse. How does it resonate with you?

> "Brethren, I count not myself to have apprehended: but this one thing I do, forgetting those things which are behind, and reaching forth unto those things which are before, I press toward the mark for the prize of the high calling of God in Christ Jesus." (Philippians 3:13-14, KJV)

Journal Prompts

As you journey through the process of making peace with your past and finding purpose in the present, take a moment to reflect on the following questions:

What aspects of your past are still causing you pain or holding you back? _____

_____
_____
_____
_____
_____
_____
_____
_____
_____
_____
_____

How have these experiences shaped your present beliefs and actions? _____

_____
_____
_____
_____
_____
_____
_____
_____
_____
_____
_____
_____
_____
_____

What steps can you take to heal from the wounds of the past and embrace the present with renewed purpose? _____

_____
_____
_____
_____
_____
_____
_____
_____
_____
_____
_____
_____
_____
_____

Prayer

Dear Lord,

As I reflect on the journey of making peace with my past and embracing the present, I come before you seeking healing and guidance. Help me release the pain and burdens of the past, knowing that you are my ultimate source of redemption. Grant me the strength and courage to face any unresolved issues, to forgive myself and others, and to find healing in your loving arms.

I surrender my past to you, Lord, and I ask for your wisdom to navigate the path ahead. Open my heart to your divine purpose for my life, and grant me the clarity and courage to embrace it fully. Thank you for your constant presence and guidance throughout this transformative journey.

In Jesus' name, I pray.

Amen.

As we peer into the distance, we will see a beautiful table that stretches beyond our sight. There is a seat at that table with our name on it, saved specifically for us. We won't have to fight for it or question our belonging.
We can rest in the glorious love of God.

EPILOGUE

Reflections and Steps on Your Journey to Healing

During the process of writing this book, I encountered numerous spiritual storms in my own life that brought deep pain to the surface. God revealed to me behaviors, thoughts, patterns, and habits that were hindering me from fully embodying his purpose for me.

I firmly believe that the enemy recognizes the incredible power this book holds, especially for those women who need it the most. Guess what? You have a story within you that needs to be told too. Perhaps you may never share it on a stage or in a book, but somewhere out there, someone is eagerly waiting for you to make peace with your pain and embrace it as part of your present purpose. Your story, your light, and your love could be exactly what that person needs.

So, let's dive deep into the root of it, sister. Why is it essential for you to SHOW UP, and why is NOW the time?

Because you were specifically chosen for this very moment. There are people out there who desperately need you. Every mistake, every experience, and every encounter with Jesus has prepared you to be his hands and feet. God needs you to show up and be his physical representation on this earth. You might wonder, "Why should I be different? There are already so many people demonstrating the love of Christ." The answer is simple: He created you uniquely, and there is only one you.

But how can you do this? First and foremost, immerse yourself in God's Word. Seek him in prayer and surround yourself with godly mentors. As you are filled, go and pour out what God has given you onto others.

Take care of yourself. Dive deep into self-discovery and understand why you do what you do. Identify the barriers holding you back and begin the healing process. When you start to heal and set healthy boundaries, you will be able to fully embrace the work God has called you to do.

While God is the ultimate expert healer, he often places people in our lives to assist us. Pray for godly mentorship and seek professional help if necessary. I believe in the power of an anointed church using oil to anoint and pray over you as you heal. For years, I sought physical healing at the altar for various illnesses, but one day God prompted me to ask for spiritual healing from my pain and trauma. Sometimes, he grants instant healing, while other times we must persist and continue asking, seeking, and knocking. It requires us to exercise our faith. Ask him to lead you to the right people and guide you in your healing journey. Surrender everything to him.

Eliminate any distractions that hinder you from severing ties with pain and hinder you from walking in God's purpose. Reflect on what you turn to when things go wrong. Is it food? Addictions? Gossip? Love from others? These distractions keep us from finding true comfort in God and can become idols if we're not careful. Assess your life and ask God, as well as yourself, what needs to be let go. Even if you are engaged in good things, they may be preventing you from experiencing his best for you.

Learn to say no and wait for God's guidance in all aspects of your life. This is crucial in the healing process. Your peace must be safeguarded, and healthy boundaries are essential. Work daily on retraining your brain and thoughts. Take your thoughts captive and recognize the power of thinking about your thinking.

Be proactive. Understand that the enemy is like a lion, seeking to devour you. But remember, he is "like" a lion; he is not a lion himself. He is merely a copycat. You already know his tactics and what he uses to trip you up. How can you take action beforehand? How can you prepare yourself for the battle? Read Ephesians and put on your spiritual armor daily. Adversity will continue to arise in your life, as it is part of the enemy's plan. He will attempt to steal your voice, peace, and joy.

If you have a willing and receptive heart, God will use you. Don't underestimate small beginnings. Remember Tully's story? Remember when she heard that verse about Jesus?

Stop allowing Satan to convince you that you are not good enough or that you cannot be used by God. Stop letting him steal your voice, your identity, and your blessings. Stop letting the enemy rob you of your authority.

Seek the gifts of the Spirit, particularly through discernment and prayer. Become a prayer warrior. Ask God to help you in these areas.

Allow yourself to be filled. Whatever you need to give up and sacrifice to be filled, do it. Surrender it all to God and wholeheartedly say, "Jesus, you can have it all." He will take every broken piece of your sincere offering and use it for his purpose.

Make the Father's business your top priority. Your mission is to KNOW HIM and to make Him KNOWN.

Show up as your perfectly imperfect self. People will relate to your imperfections more than if you attempt to portray an image of perfection.

Seek the Kingdom of God first in everything you do, and all else will fall into place.

Every single morning, seek God's guidance in every aspect of your life. Pray for your spiritual growth, your relationships, your work, your decisions—everything.

Remember, dear sister, this healing journey is not a solitary one. God is with you every step of the way, guiding, supporting, and empowering you. Trust in his unfailing love and embrace the transformative power of healing in your life. May you find joy, peace, and fulfillment as you continue your journey to becoming the woman God has called you to be.

JOURNAL REFLECTION
Beyond These Pages

Reflection

As you reach the end of this transformative journey, take a moment to reflect on the following questions.

Journal Prompts

How has this journey to discovering your true identity and finding your place at God's table changed you? _____
_____
_____
_____
_____
_____
_____
_____
_____
_____
_____
_____
_____
_____
_____
_____

Come to the Table

What are the most significant lessons you have learned along the way? _____
_____
_____
_____
_____
_____
_____
_____
_____
_____
_____
_____

How will you carry these newfound insights and experiences into your future? _____
_____
_____
_____
_____
_____
_____
_____
_____
_____
_____
_____
_____
_____
_____

How can you make peace with the past and find purpose in the present? _____
_____
_____
_____
_____
_____
_____
_____
_____
_____
_____

How can you begin to tell or write your own story? How do you think it will help you in the healing process? _____
_____
_____
_____
_____
_____
_____
_____
_____
_____
_____
_____

"For I know the thoughts that I think toward you, saith the LORD, thoughts of peace, and not of evil, to give you an expected end." (Jeremiah 29:11, KJV)

Prayer

Heavenly Father,

As I come to the end of this transformative journey, I am filled with gratitude for the work you have done in my life. Thank you for guiding me to the truth of who I am and showing me my rightful place at your table.

Lord, I reflect on the lessons learned, the healing experienced, and the growth that has taken place within me. I am in awe of your faithfulness and the plans you have for me, plans that bring prosperity, hope, and a future filled with purpose.

I commit to carrying these newfound insights into my everyday life. Help me to live out my true identity as your beloved child, to walk in confidence, and to fulfill the purpose you have ordained for me.

Thank you for the journey you have taken me on, for the healing and restoration you have brought to my life. May your presence continue to guide and strengthen me as I embark on the next chapter of my story.

In Jesus' name, I pray.

Amen.

Scripture to Meditate Upon:

Psalm 139:14 (KJV) — "I will praise thee; for I am fearfully and wonderfully made: marvellous are thy works; and that my soul knoweth right well."

Ephesians 2:10 (KJV) — "For we are his workmanship, created in Christ Jesus unto good works, which God hath before ordained that we should walk in them."

Isaiah 61:1 (KJV) — "The Spirit of the Lord God is upon me; because the Lord hath anointed me to preach good tidings unto the meek; he hath sent me to bind up the brokenhearted, to proclaim liberty to the captives, and the opening of the prison to them that are bound."

2 Corinthians 5:17 (KJV) — "Therefore if any man be in Christ, he is a new creature: old things are passed away; behold, all things are become new."

Romans 8:37 (KJV) — "Nay, in all these things we are more than conquerors through him that loved us."

Jeremiah 29:11 (KJV) — "For I know the thoughts that I think toward you, saith the Lord, thoughts of peace, and not of evil, to give you an expected end."

Matthew 11:28–30 (KJV) — "Come unto me, all ye that labour and are heavy laden, and I will give you rest. Take my yoke upon you, and learn of me; for I am meek and lowly in heart: and ye shall find rest unto your souls. For my yoke is easy, and my burden is light."

Philippians 4:13 (KJV) — "I can do all things through Christ which strengtheneth me."

Psalm 23:1 (KJV) — "The Lord is my shepherd; I shall not want."

1 Peter 5:7 (KJV) — "Casting all your care upon him; for he careth for you."

Isaiah 43:18–19 (KJV) — "Remember ye not the former things, neither consider the things of old. Behold, I will do a new thing; now it shall spring forth; shall ye not know it? I will even make a way in the wilderness, and rivers in the desert."

Romans 12:2 (KJV) — "And be not conformed to this world: but be ye transformed by the renewing of your mind, that ye may prove what is that good, and acceptable, and perfect, will of God."

Psalm 34:17–18 (KJV) — "The righteous cry, and the Lord heareth, and delivereth them out of all their troubles. The Lord is nigh unto them that are of a broken heart; and saveth such as be of a contrite spirit."

Isaiah 41:10 (KJV) — "Fear thou not; for I am with thee: be not dismayed; for I am thy God: I will strengthen thee; yea, I will help thee; yea, I will uphold thee with the right hand of my righteousness."

Romans 8:28 (KJV) — "And we know that all things work together for good to them that love God, to them who are the called according to his purpose."

Your story, your voice,
and your journey matter.

BONUS CHAPTER

Writing Your Own Story of Healing and Redemption

"And they have conquered him by the blood of the Lamb and by the word of their testimony…" (Revelation 12:11a, KJV)

Sister friend, thank you for joining me on this transformative journey of healing and self-discovery through *Come to the Table: Healing from the Past, Discovering Purpose in the Present*. As you've delved into the pages of this book, you've encountered powerful stories, affirmations, and scriptures that have hopefully lit a spark of hope in you.

Now, it's time to use that spark to ignite your own story—a story of healing, redemption, and faith.

Step 1: Reflect on Your Journey

Before you put pen to paper, take some time to reflect on your own journey. Think about the moments in your life when you've felt broken, burdened, or silenced by past hurts. Write down your thoughts, feelings, and memories. Allow yourself to acknowledge the pain and the longing for healing. Remember, healing begins with honesty and self-awareness.

Step 2: Embrace God's Promises

Refer to the scriptures you've encountered in this book and any others that resonate with you. The Word of God is a powerful source of inspiration. Choose scriptures that speak to your journey of healing and redemption. For example:

- Psalm 34:18 (KJV): "The Lord is nigh unto them that are of a broken heart; and saveth such as be of a contrite spirit."
- Isaiah 43:18–19 (KJV): "I will even make a way in the wilderness, and rivers in the desert."

Step 3: Identify Your Unique Story

Consider the unique aspects of your journey. What makes your story special and worth sharing? Think about the challenges you've faced, the lessons you've learned, and the transformation you've experienced. Your story is one of a kind, and it has the potential to inspire and impact others.

Step 4: Write Your Testimony

Begin writing your testimony. Share your story honestly and authentically. Talk about the pain, the obstacles, and the moments of doubt. Describe how you encountered God's love, grace, and healing. Share the turning points in your journey—the moments when you felt God's presence and guidance most profoundly.

Step 5: Offer Hope and Encouragement

As you write, focus on offering hope and encouragement to others who may be going through similar struggles. Share how your faith sustained you, and how God's promises became a source of strength. Your story can be a lifeline for someone else.

Step 6: Seek Support and Accountability

Writing your story can be an emotional process. Don't hesitate to seek support from friends, family, or a support group. Share your progress with someone you trust, and ask for their encouragement and accountability.

Step 7: Edit and Revise

After you've written your story, take the time to edit and revise it. Make sure it flows well and communicates your message clearly. Allow the Holy Spirit to help you with this process. Ask a trusted mentor and friend to review it for you.

Step 8: Pray Over Your Testimony

Pray over your testimony, asking God to use it for His glory. Invite His presence to be with you as you share your story with others. Remember that your testimony has the potential to touch hearts and draw people closer to God.

Step 9: Share Your Story

Once your testimony is ready, look for opportunities to share it. This could be in your church, a small group, or even through writing platforms or social media. Your story has the power to inspire, heal, and bring hope to others.

Step 10: Keep Writing

Your story doesn't end here. Continue to write about your journey, your ongoing growth, and your relationship with God. Use your writing as a tool for personal healing and for reaching out to others.

Remember, your story is a testament to God's love and faithfulness. By sharing it, you become a living example of

Revelation 12:11a. Your words have the power to conquer darkness and bring light into the lives of others.

May your writing journey be blessed, and may you continue to find healing, purpose, and fulfillment in Christ as you share your story with the world.

One day I hope to see all of you
at our Father's table.

Love,
Tabitha

Made in the USA
Columbia, SC
20 June 2025